T0287660

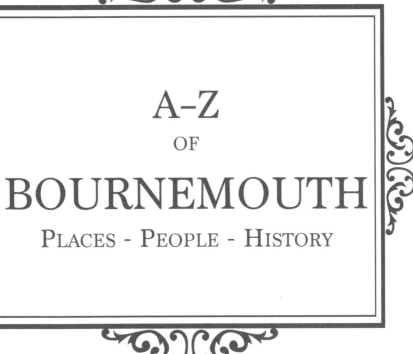

A–Z

OF

BOURNEMOUTH

PLACES - PEOPLE - HISTORY

W. A. Hoodless

AMBERLEY

Acknowledgements

Although the history of the relatively recent town of Bournemouth is already considerably documented, it is well worth taking a fresh look using the A–Z format and including numerous illustrations not previously published.

Many are either by the author, assigned to the author or out of copyright. Where appropriate, attribution is given by naming the illustration's supplier in brackets after the caption. Special thanks are due to Alwyn Ladell for permission to select from his excellent collection. The author and publisher would also like to thank, in no particular order, the following people/organisations for their kind permission to use copyright and other material in this book: Mrs Julia Smith, Mrs Myrna Chave, Janet Burn, Bruce Lawson, Nigel Beale, Grant Rayner, Christopher Hollick, Judith Dobie, Michael Stead, Steve Robson, D. L. Chalk, Bournemouth Transport Ltd, Heritage Collection Bournemouth Library, Jarrold Publishing & St Peter's Church, Russell-Cotes Art Gallery and Museum Bournemouth (RCAGM), *Dorset Life*, Moordown Halifax Memorial, Pixabay, Charles Rolls Heritage Trust, National Portrait Gallery London, Hornby Hobbies Ltd and St Mark's School Talbot Village.

Every attempt has been made to seek permission for copyright material used in this book. However, if we have inadvertently used copyright material without permission/acknowledgement, we apologise and will make the necessary correction at the first opportunity.

Apart from photographs, there have been various contributions in less tangible ways such as advice, encouragement, pointers and stories. My heartfelt thanks to one and all.

First published 2022

Amberley Publishing
The Hill, Stroud, Gloucestershire, GL5 4EP
www.amberley-books.com

Copyright © W. A. Hoodless, 2022

The right of W. A. Hoodless to be identified as the Author of this work has been asserted in accordance with the Copyrights, Designs and Patents Act 1988.

ISBN 978 1 4456 9894 6 (print)
ISBN 978 1 4456 9895 3 (ebook)

All rights reserved. No part of this book may be reprinted or reproduced or utilised in any form or by any electronic, mechanical or other means, now known or hereafter invented, including photocopying and recording, or in any information storage or retrieval system, without the permission in writing from the Publishers.

British Library Cataloguing in Publication Data. A catalogue record for this book is available from the British Library.

Typesetting by SJmagic DESIGN SERVICES, India. Printed in Great Britain.

Contents

Introduction

A–Z of Bournemouth describes how the fast-growing town began and what has happened, some chapters being longer than others to give more depth to particular stories.

In the early days of personal individuality, there was a strong mixture of the landed aristocracy, tradesmen and workers; settlers like Tregonwell and the Drax Grosvenors saw the tiny new village as a summer playground for themselves and their aristocratic friends. Certainly, for twenty-six years from Bournemouth's perceived foundation as a watering place in 1810, very little was developed.

After the death of the main town centre landowner Sir George Ivison Tapps in 1835, his son and heir took a different approach. He soon arranged for two new hotels, sixteen beautifully set villas in Westover Road and a church, thus beginning the culture of enterprise that is a trademark of the town to this day.

By the 1860s, ambitious businessmen had made great progress in putting this new settlement on the map. Yet despite the first town guides waxing lyrical about its beauty and charm, all was not well for everybody, as evidenced by the mid-nineteenth-century founding of Talbot Village by Georgina Talbot. She had been greatly moved by a crowd of the poor banging on the windows of her family's large house on the East Cliff, saying that they were starving and needed work.

Having initially been a select retreat for the rich, the growing village now targeted those well-off but unwell, becoming a premier health resort particularly for people with chest complaints. Next, the fast rail connection arrived, bringing with it hordes of day-trippers in season and horrifying many of the well-to-do residents.

By 1900, Bournemouth was a fully established going concern that had taken full advantage of its natural attributes, not least the sun, sea and sand. Twentieth-century growth and modernisation continued relentlessly. Perhaps today after the merger of the town with Christchurch and Poole on 1 April 2019, there is even less hesitation about demolition and redevelopment should decision makers deem a scheme to be desirable.

Curiously, both of the letters A and Z cover tragic events.

Avenue Road Tram Disaster

In 1897, the British Electric Tram Company suggested a scheme that was vigorously opposed by the Corporation, which claimed that trams were unsuitable for the town. However, progress was not to be denied and five years later, the Corporation had its own system linking the Lansdowne with Pokesdown and the town centre with Westbourne.

The tragedy at Avenue Road was found to be the result of an inherent fault with the design of the brakes. On 1 May 1908, tramcar 72 gathered speed as it travelled downhill towards The Square, but after the brakes failed, control was lost, seven were killed and twenty-six seriously injured.

According to a report about a sale of heritage postcards, the auctioneer commented:

> My grandfather also happens to be an eyewitness to the event. He was six years old at the time and was living above Cullens grocery which his father ran in the Triangle, next to The Branksome Arms. He remembered the screeching and unbelievable noise of the tram as it sped by, as the brakes had already failed by then and it was picking up considerable speed.

Popular macabre postcard of tram tragedy.

Battle of Wick and Tuckton: A Reminiscence from Nineteenth-century Southbourne

Richard Dale, born around 1795 at Stourfield House in Southbourne, provided his recollections for publication in 1876 when he was described as an 'aged farmer with a bright memory'. The house was built in 1766 by Edmund Bott and described by Richard as the 'first mansion on the common between Christchurch Head and Poole'. He gave some fascinating insights such as the old saying in the county about smuggling: 'Ill-gotten wealth is slippery and cannot be held'.

The battle was between two local men fighting for the hand of a lady's maid to the kindly and popular Mrs Bott. In Richard's own words:

> It happened that she was in favour with two swains, who agreed to fight a battle at Tuckton Cross, and winner of the battle to have and to hold the nymph for life, and a long life she had at the cottage near the pond at Iford. She breathed her last at the age of ninety-five years. Her husband died about twelve years previously. His name was Charles Pain. He told me that the battle was a hard fought one, and many were there to see it. One of the combatants lived at Tuckton, and the other, the successful one at Wick. When I was a child it was a common remark to hear the boys saying, when at play in the evening:

> 'A battle was fought at Tuckton Cross,
> Where Wick won and Tuckton lost'.

Beach Huts

The chance of using a beach hut has been one of the resort's prime attractions since the UK's first municipal one was installed in 1909. Complete with a blue plaque, it is still there to the east of the pier and numbered 2359.

One's very own timber shed by the sea.

The holidaymaker's great benefit is the sheltered and private base from which they can enjoy the sea and sands, a major improvement on the Victorian bathing machines, which had to be wheeled into the water.

Along the promenades, there are some 1,400 hut sites licensed to residents who each must pay an annual site fee, at the time of writing of more than £1,000. The resident must first reach the top of a long and slowly moving waiting list and then provide and maintain his or her own hut. Alternatively, anyone can hire a hut directly from its owner or pay for a council hut by the day or week.

Apart from using it for getting changed and storing deckchairs, there is access to a nearby tap for drinking water and a gas ring is permitted. Indeed, not only can tea be made but whole meals can be cooked. Beach lodges and pods are even more luxurious. Just about the only downside, apart from cost, is occasional damage by winter storms.

Bennett, Alexander Morden: Churchman of Energy and Enthusiasm

As the first vicar of St Peter's Church, newly consecrated in 1845, Revd A. M. Bennett (1808–80) knew that he was taking on a major task needing great resolution of purpose. At that time, there was neither parsonage nor school with the living.

Starting with a reportedly ugly church seating 300, already too small for the growing town, he not only enlarged it in phases until the 202-feet-high spire was completed in 1879, but avoided debt by funding all extensions in advance. Over time, Bennett transformed it into a most elegant and attractive place of worship. Moreover, he worked extremely hard as a sort of religious developer of new churches, chapels and church schools in Westbourne, Pokesdown, Moordown, East Cliff, East Parley, Branksome Park and St Michael's Road.

Thus, in addition to being a parish vicar for some thirty-five years while holding a number of chaplaincies, he was often consulting with his friend, the architect G. E. Street, to organise substantial building works.

Bennett, who was given to uncompromising sermons about sin and redemption, proved ideal for the challenging living, being austere, duty-minded, determined and highly respected. The vicar's efforts were so extensive, untiring and indeed appreciated that St Stephen's Church, also known as the Bennett Memorial Church, was funded by public subscription and built in his honour and remembrance.

Reverend Alexander Morden Bennett
1808 · 1880
Founder of Churches and Schools

St Peter's Church. *Inset*: Pavilion plaque honouring first Bournemouth vicar A. M. Bennett.

Nave of St Peter's Church. (© Jarrold Publishing & St Peter's Church)

Boscombe's Growth

The earliest mention of Boscombe may be in the maps by Norden (1607), Speed (1611) and Bowen (1720): a Bascambe Copperas House. The mineral pyrite, or 'fool's gold', was used for manufacturing copperas, which is hydrated ferrous sulphate also known as green vitriol for making ink. No sign of this industry remains.

Much later, as a heathland common, Boscombe saw its population soar from twenty-seven in 1841, 282 in 1871, 1,895 in 1881, 6,324 in 1891 to 9,648 in 1901. The earliest census identified just seventeen at Boscombe House (now Shelley Park) and ten at three cottages.

Suitable housing, in locations like Boscombe, was urgently needed for the builders and the many tradespeople servicing Bournemouth. By 1900, Boscombe was mainly developed south of Boscombe and Pokesdown Stations while the low-density houses of the Portman Estate and Boscombe Manor were still to be built.

Some other elements of this strong new suburb of Bournemouth were the Grand Theatre for some 2,000 (now O2 Academy), the Royal Arcade, 160,000-gallon water tower, various schools, shops, halls, hospitals and churches. A quickly created community with its own identity.

Shelley Park, Boscombe, including the medical centre, Percy Florence Shelley's theatre and apartments.

Trams, horses and the Royal Arcade on Christchurch Road, Boscombe, 1911. (Alwyn Ladell)

Boscombe Seafront

Before Boscombe started to develop in the 1860s, the heathland was desolate indeed. South of a line from Wentworth Avenue to Owls Road, there is now the municipally managed clifftop and Chine Gardens, Boscombe Overcliff Drive, the Chine Hotel, the mainly interwar low-density housing and a variety of apartment blocks.

   The well-promoted spa, covered by a thatched roof, dating from around 1870 and having the benefit of a drinking fountain installed by the Earl of Malmesbury, was one element of Boscombe's competition with the town centre. Enough Victorians believed in the medicinal qualities of natural mineral water to make such spas highly desirable and the more unpleasant the flavour, the more good it must be doing! Being a chalybeate spring, it tasted of iron salts. Sea Road and Boscombe Chine gave convenient access to the beach for sea air and bathing while the nearby spa, which became a fashionable meeting place, lasted until the 1920s. The 1872 OS map shows 'Boscombe Mouth' but it never caught on as a name.

What is now the Chine Hotel was opened in 1874, the Chine Gardens were mainly laid out in the 1880s, the first pier was completed by 1889 and the enormous Burlington Hotel (now flats) was completed in 1893. The present pier, breached for defence reasons in 1940, was reconstructed with reinforced concrete, reopening in 1962 and since slimmed down by the removal of the Mermaid Theatre in the refurbishment of 2008. Two years later, it won the Pier of the Year award.

Spa and Chine Hotel, 1876. (Alwyn Ladell)

Spa in its early twentieth-century setting. (Alwyn Ladell)

Today's mirrored globe, two granite blocks and replica spa shelter.

Boscombe's elegant pier and children's climbing rocks.

Bourne Mouth in 1810

Although over 200 years have passed since most of the land between Poole and Christchurch was a heath, a certain healthy tension remains between each of them and Bournemouth. Indeed, some still see it as a fast-grown upstart despite the merger in April 2019 of the three boroughs.

The Brook is shown on the map as a tiny river running through marshy ground at the bottom of the shallow valley and meandering to the east at the coastline, the meander being caused by the prevailing eastwards longshore drift of the sands.

The town centre, but in 1810! (Michael Stead and Bournemouth Library)

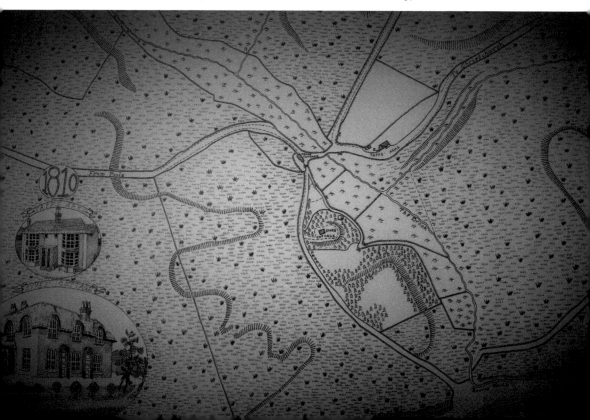

In 1810, some important routes were already in place, including what is now Poole Road, Exeter Road, Bath Road, Old Christchurch Road and Wimborne Road. Decoy Pond Cottage and the Tapps Arms were both smugglers' haunts, which are today the locations of Bobby's (formerly Debenhams) and the junction of Old Christchurch Road with Post Office Road respectively. Ashley Villa was near to the Tapps Arms and Bourne House adjoined the cottage. A tributary of the Brook ran parallel to Old Christchurch Road but that has long since been culverted under Beales and The Arcade.

Of special note is Symes' Cottage (named after Tregonwell's butler who is believed by many to have been a smuggler), described under its subsequent name of Portman Lodge later in the book. As for the Tapps Arms, it was destined to be destroyed by fire in 1821 and rebuilt by Lewis as the Tregonwell Arms.

Bourne Stream Source

'Large streams from little fountains flow,
Tall oaks from little acorns grow'

David Everett

The stream is a small river that has nonetheless given its name to arguably the best seaside resort in the country. Certainly, it looks beautiful and quaint as it runs down through the Upper, Middle and Lower Gardens.

First visible trace of Bournemouth's famous river: three culvert outfalls at Ringwood Road.

To the north-west of Coy Pond, its line continues upstream through Poole and the shallow Bourne Valley catchment until it reaches the Ringwood Road dual carriageway.

The source is threefold, comprising surface water from roads, the Francis Road waterworks site and Canford Heath. Three culverts take it under Ringwood Road to feed Bourne Bottom. Scenic it is not.

Bourne Valley on 28 October 1819: Drawing by Mrs M. A. T. Whitby

Until photography first became effective around 1860, there were few illustrations of the area in those early days.

An exception occurred when amateur artist Mrs Whitby travelled and drew some of the south coast in 1819, visiting the carefully located Mansion and doing a pencil outline from the drawing room. It is one of two on page 23 of the album, probably being the first known showing the sea end of Bourne Valley; the other was done from the dining room and dated at the top of the same page.

When viewing what is now the Lower Gardens and Pier Approach, she sketched the Isle of Wight and St Catherine's Point on the horizon together with a small summerhouse towards the foot of the East Cliff. There were also boats, rustic benches and wheeled bathing huts.

The drawing was seven years after the Mansion was first occupied as a summer residence but that superb 1819 sea view is no more, being almost totally obstructed by buildings.

Outlook from Tregonwell's house down Bourne Valley. (Mrs Julia Smith)

Branksome Dene Murder

In 1946, the mutilated body of Doreen Marshall was discovered near a rhododendron bush in Branksome Dene Chine.

Surprisingly, the suspected killer, Neville Heath, was an ex-Bomber Command pilot who had once been shot down and reportedly bailed out last in order to save the lives of his crew. His guilt for this murder was generally assumed after his arrest in Bournemouth for a previous murder in the London hotel of actress Margery Gardner. He had booked into a Bournemouth hotel on the West Cliff as Group Captain Rupert Brook.

Although a charming and handsome war hero and a good pilot, Heath's trial revealed a sadist who led a life of deception. He was executed at Pentonville Prison on 16 October 1946.

Apart from several aliases, deceptions included stealing an RAF officer's car, forging cheques in Cairo and wearing medals to which he was not entitled in South Africa, thus creating a record of three courts martial. He was seconded to Bomber Command from the South African Air Force to carry out bombing missions over occupied Europe, leaving behind his young wife Elizabeth and son. After the war, he returned to her, but got divorced in return for £2,000 paid by her family. The year 1946 found him in London mixing with petty criminals and prostitutes.

Intriguingly, although there seemed little doubt about Heath's guilt in the Branksome Dene case, he was only taken to court for the murder of Margery Gardner. Right to the end, he was very calm about the pending execution. When asked if he would like a tot of whisky, the reply was 'In view of the circumstances, old boy, you'd better make that a double!'

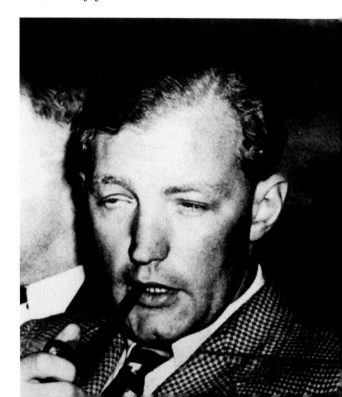

Murderer Neville Heath.
(Bournemouth Library)

Camera Obscura Café in The Square

The first-floor Camera Obscura, meaning 'dark room' in Latin, is above the ground-level Café Obscura, which was built in 1999 over the Bourne Stream and old tram rails. When the circular room is darkened by blinds to its sloping windows, a fascinating moving image in colour can be projected vertically downwards on to a white image table.

The clock, which used to be in the middle of the former huge roundabout and before that at the tramways waiting room from 1925, has been installed at the top of the building but with one clock face replaced by glass. The café and clock with its glass face can be seen in the photograph illustrating today's Square.

Similar to a periscope, the light is reflected down by a mirror to a lens and then to the white table, which can be raised or lowered to achieve focus. The whole clock is rotated by remote control. It is fascinating to see the moving panorama of The Square and its surrounding area in full colour as the clock turns round, no doubt surprising pedestrians outside.

The image produced is filled with luminous delicate colours capturing the ever-moving outside scene.

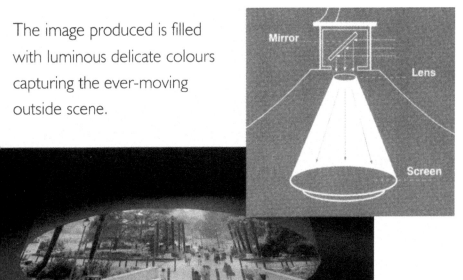

Camera Obscura in action. Sketch, darkened room and image table. (Grant Rayner)

C

Centenary Fêtes of July 1910: Unacceptable Risk for the Town or Great Commercial Opportunity?

In 1909, the Publicity Committee was advised that the town's foundation year was 1810 when the Tregonwells visited and Lewis bought building land.

This became the justification for a huge Bournemouth-promoting celebration, which included Britain's first International Aviation Meeting, fancy dress masked balls, parades, musical events, quarter deck balls on the pier, float competitions, grotesque carnivals, a grand dramatic display by 2,000 boys, motor boat races, battles of flowers, large-scale town centre decorations, fireworks, military tattoo, naval tournament, night-time illuminations in the town centre and even a house burned down in a fire brigade display.

Despite the financial risk to the Corporation-supported company being covered by a guarantee fund of £30,000, not all were happy. The *Graphic* even had a cartoon with miserable Little Johnnie throwing the mud of sarcasm against Mr Bournemouth and the Fêtes, but John Bull gave Little Johnnie short shrift. Thanks to six months' hard work by 340 people, promotional success was achieved, though sadly the Aviation Meeting was marred by the fatal accident of Charles Rolls, co-founder of Rolls-Royce.

Success! Chairman of Centenary Fêtes, F. J. Bell, attracts the big spenders.

Fashionable elegance and newfangled aviation on the English Riviera.

Centenary competition float. Rostand's French romantic play starring farmyard animals. (Alwyn Ladell)

Coat of Arms and Crest

The town's coat of arms was granted on 24 March 1891 after borough status was achieved the previous year. The highest feature, above four English roses, is a pine tree symbolising the town's parks and gardens.

The azure and 'or' (gold) colours of the shield are the same as for the royal arms of the Saxon king Edward the Confessor (1003–66), the royal estate then including the present area of the town.

Above the shield, supporting the crest, is the helm, being a helmet that knights would wear in battle. The shield has a cross flory, being a cross with a three-petal *fleur de lis* (lilly) at each of the four ends of the cross. The setting is a wreath of the colours, referring to the azure and 'or' above.

In the first and third quarters is a lion rampant holding the Hampshire rose, representing readiness to defend against sea attack.

The second quarter has six martlets, heraldic birds without legs because they are in perpetual flight. They may also relate to the sand martins of the cliffs.

The fourth quarter has four salmon symbolising the fish in the River Stour, which marks the boundary with Christchurch.

The motto '*Pulchritudo et Salubritas*', translates as beauty and health to represent the reason for the town's existence.

Bournemouth coat of arms and crest.
(Alwyn Ladell)

Commons and Unofficial Houses: Family Reminiscence from Robert Starks

Starks (1845–1922) worked on a farm, then for ten years in the Navy and at thirty-five, settled in Boscombe as a coachman, becoming a verger and chorister at St James' Church, Pokesdown. During his boyhood, his father explained how people learnt to 'make a home', no doubt describing a custom from around 1800 or earlier. In Robert's own words:

The way people used to get their own house on the common was to buy or get in some way an old wagon, a farm wagon for preference as they was generally bigger than other vehicles. Anyway, after they had got the wagon they would build a house on it with hurdles and a chimney with bricks and clay and cover the hurdles with rushes and mud to keep the place dry. Then after they had got everything ready on some moonlit night (after they had prospected around and found a plot to their liking) they then would get some men and horses and haul the house to the piece of ground.

Then after the house had been put in (where sometime or other it would be enlarged) the fire would be lit and the pot put on, and always after the house had been permanently built the fire had to be kept burning and the pot hung over it, but during the time they were fixing the wagon most of the men was busy marking out the garden by turning up a spit of turf right round the piece of ground, and, of course, in after years as time rolled on by throwing up the bank outside they made the plot larger. The house – by getting clay out of the plot they made mud and mixed straw or some other stuff with the mud and built their cottage around the old one on wheels. My father used to say it made a lot of hard work, but the women and all the family had a hand in it. Well after they had got the roof on they dismantled the old wagon, and finished their cottage at leisure, and I can assure you that most of these mud cottages was nice and warm in the winter with their big chimney corners.

Cooper Deans: Unsung Benefactors to the Town

Bournemouth has gained enormously from the generosity of certain families, perhaps none more so than the Cooper Deans, who originated as the Deans, yeomen farmers of Holdenhurst.

John Dean, who married well and aspired to improve his lot, bought a 56-acre holding, Little Down, in 1771 and sold it for profit in 1772. It was repurchased in 1798 by John's son, surgeon turned banker William Dean, who immediately built Littledown House, now part of JPMorgan Chase. It may later have helped the family that William's son-in-law William Clapcott was one of the three Inclosure Commissioners who, in 1805, allotted William Dean 1,137 acres of what is now mostly prime town land. The future was set fair.

The 1825 stock market crash affected a bank that Clapcott directed and which failed in 1826, leaving his widow Mary and son, another William, to struggle with heavily mortgaged land. But Mary, not trusting her husband's rather rash nature, had wisely taken out life policies when times were good. On her death in 1854, his son William received a surprise insurance payment of £16,500, enough to clear the debts.

From this time, when Bournemouth really began to expand, the generosity of the family became a real boon to the town, one which continued to the death in 1984 of its last member, Ellen Cooper Dean. Outright gifts or disposals on nominal terms were legion. A few examples must suffice: sites for Wimborne Road Cemetery, Firs Home Sanatorium, West Cliff nursing home, Baptist Church Lansdowne, St Paul's School, St Michael's School, Dean Park Cricket Ground, Royal Victoria Hospital, Dean Court Football Ground and public open space at West Overcliff Drive. Even the present main railway station was built on Dean land.

William died in 1887 and was succeeded by his cousin James Edward Cooper (1840–1921), a builder from York. Sadly, as a rich widower, James could not remarry in 1895 as he wished because a resettlement deed was required, which would have disadvantaged his son and heir Joseph. When Joseph refused to agree to the deed, it proved the writing on the wall for the end of the dynasty because there were no more children. Both of Joseph's daughters Ellen (1899–1984) and Edith (1902–77) died as spinsters without issue. Meanwhile, between the wars, a lot of development land was sold to pay heavy death duties following the death of James. Joseph lived until 1950, passing the estate to Ellen and Edith.

It remains to mention perhaps the biggest benefaction of all: a 136-acre site including Littledown House. It was sold to the council by the sisters for a modest £2.64 million in 1973, payable over eight years without interest and possession to be given in 1984. Together with another site, which was also sold, it meant that the council did well by selling on for both housing and to the bank, now JPMorgan Chase, for their European headquarters. Moreover, the council could build the Littledown Centre in its 47 acres of parkland. Ellen's charity, set up in 1977 with widely drawn objects, now has assets of some £34 million. A truly benevolent family.

Left: James Edward Cooper continued the family's generosity to Bournemouth.

Below: The Cooper Dean sisters provided considerable parkland for Bournemouth's Leisure Centre.

Christopher Crabb Creeke:
Surveyor and Inspector of Nuisances
'Father of Bournemouth'

Born in Cambridge the son of a tailor, Creeke (1820–86) became an architect and surveyor who was responsible for hundreds of buildings in spacious plots and much of the attractive road layout. His curved avenues, with few right angles, were often lined with bushes while road junctions were enhanced by stands of trees. He improved substandard roads, installed street lighting and provided a good water supply and drainage system.

Having helped to promote the Bournemouth Improvement Act of 1856, this forceful personality held the meetings of the new Commissioners in the dining room of his house, Lainston Villa, by The Square, until a town hall was built to his design in 1875.

Other designs included the Boscombe Manor extensions, which first brought him to Bournemouth, Wimborne Road cemetery and chapel, first Congregational Church on Richmond Hill, central Post Office, extensions to the Bath Hotel and work for the Dean, West Cliff and Durrant estates. Somehow, Creeke found time to supervise the laying out of Pleasure Gardens and to be captain of the first rifle corps.

In 1881, he resigned as surveyor due to a 'culture of individualism' among board members regarding his main drainage scheme but, two years later, was elected a Commissioner at the head of the poll.

There was a large procession at his funeral with some 1,000 gathered at the cemetery while shops closed and the bell of St Peter's Church tolled. When presenting an oil painting of Creeke to the Commissioners, Joseph Cutler emphasised that he worked for the town and not his own advantage, and expressed his wish that present and future representatives would find this likeness an incentive to honest duty. Was there a message here?

Today, the contribution to the town of this tireless man is recognised by a Pavilion plaque and in a humorous sculpture in the front grounds of the Bournemouth International Centre. Sombre and lost in thought, he sits on a WC, back to back with a smiling Lewis Tregonwell, who faces Exeter Road.

Christopher Crabb Creeke, Surveyor and Inspector of Nuisances. By W. J. Warren. (RCAGM)

Ducks and Smugglers at The Square: Precursor of the Village of Bourne

In 1697, Clarendon (lord of the manor) leased 25 acres at Bourne Bottom to seven men for ninety-nine years 'for duckoy', meaning to make a decoy pond to trap birds for selling as meat. This marshy ground ran from the sea to beyond the present crossing of the Bourne Stream by the Wessex Way, being an 'inclosure' which stopped commoners using it for turf cutting or grazing. The rent was one shilling p.a. plus one seventh of annual profits. Drainage ditches appear to have been installed and by 1722, the Bourn Plank crossed The Brook.

Two adjoining dwellings were built on part of the present Bobby's site: Bourne House (in 1718 occupied by preventive officer Jeans) and Decoy Pond Cottage (in 1740 occupied by pond man Harris, the partnership of seven having been dissolved). Shallow decoy ponds would have screened and covered ditches running out from the sides in order to trap lured birds. Later in the eighteenth century, there was wildfowling of ducks and geese. The decoy man would maintain everything and serve shooting and trapping parties.

In 1749, Harris was imprisoned for smuggling but later joined the customs side, as did his son. Yet by 1789, Decoy Pond Cottage was occupied by Beak, a violent smuggler who appeared to be too busy to maintain the pond which had fallen into disuse.

In 1796, Matcham took over Bourne House and suggested to lord of the manor Tapps that he should build an inn by the sea as it would be popular for bathers. By 1838, duck shooting exploits from Decoy Pond Cottage must have stopped because the two dwellings had been converted to a temporary church for the growing village of Bourne.

E

Echo

On 20 August 1900, when the first edition was produced in a former drill hall behind a butcher's shop in Holdenhurst Road, the *Echo* had the marketing benefit of paper boys asking morning customers if they would also like an evening delivery. One report that day concerned Romulus, a Spanish athlete who successfully wrestled a bull to the ground at a circus in Seville. The crowd was delighted.

By 1908, production had relocated to Albert Road using premises at the north corner with Old Christchurch Road. Over a weekend in January 1934, a final move was made to the striking new and purpose-built Echo Building, Richmond Hill.

This Grade II listed structure, a most prominent example of Bath stone art deco, was again outgrown by 1960, leading to the purchase of the adjoining New Royal Theatre and substantial internal building works. A new basement and uphill ramp allowed delivery vans to enter at Albert Road and exit into Yelverton Road, thus avoiding the unsatisfactory journey round the block. Two more 130-ton presses were added to the existing two 80-ton ones and 300 tons of newsprint could now be stored, the whole upgrade being completed in 1962.

The *Echo* has always adapted to economic and social changes that affect the demands of readers. Examples are the need for a name change from Daily to Evening in 1958, computerisation in 1987, reduced coverage of national news and the success of social media and home computing. Currently, the company only occupies part of the building, the remainder being transformed into a shared workspace complex.

Echo (1934), Catholic Church (1873), Bristol and West House (1958), Hilton (2015).

Ferrey, Benjamin: First Town Planner

Articled to the eminent Augustus Charles Pugin, Christchurch-born Ferrey (1810–80) became a talented London-based architect who produced excellent drawings of the priory church. In 1836, Sir George Tapps-Gervis asked him to design an ambitious layout for the Gervis estate in Bourne, an early form of town planning for a marine resort and the forerunner to his career as a church architect.

Since much of the land to the west of the Bourne Stream had already been sold to Tregonwell by Sir George's father, Ferrey produced drawings for the area to the east. Some of his initial proposals were carried out by 1838, notably the Bath Hotel and sixteen villas in Westover Road, thereby signalling that the tiny village really was ready for development.

However, two schemes that failed to materialise were the Pleasure Gardens Pagoda incorporating baths and assembly rooms, and a church high on the East Cliff. The

View of Bournemouth. Benjamin Ferrey's striking layout was partly achieved. (RCAGM)

first was perhaps too ambitious for its time and the Belle Vue Boarding House was built as more appropriate. As Dr Granville later pointed out, the church site was too remote and elevated for chest patients at a health resort.

Around 1845, Decimus Burton replaced Ferrey as architect to the Gervis estate. However, Ferrey's idea of a pagoda for the public was not forgotten because an 1876 lease to the Commissioners included the right to erect something similar, a pavilion. Better late than never, it was finally built in 1929.

First Beale: Founder of the Department Store Chain

John Elmes Beale (1847–1928) arrived from Weymouth in 1881 to sell toys, gifts, etc., to a fast-growing and prosperous town. The new family business, Fancy Fair, was soon part of the Bournemouth scene and he became mayor for three years from November 1902. Two descendants were also mayors in 1937 and 1978.

It was a difficult start for John and his wife Sarah, called 'Annie', who worked long hours, living in the basement of that first small shop in Old Christchurch Road. But they were popular, selling all manner of goods including tin buckets, wooden spades, dolls' dresses and Japanese sunshades. In 1885, a resident Father Christmas was introduced, immediately becoming a tradition.

Trading proved so successful that by 1886, Beale had added a three-storey extension and moved house three times, the last one to Alum Chine Road. Adjoining premises were acquired one after another, the range of goods was improved, there were more house moves, Father Christmas processions were inaugurated, premises were rebuilt and in 1923 the freehold purchased. A solid foundation had been laid for the recent chain of twenty-three stores nationwide, though sadly, difficult retail circumstances forced the company into administration in January 2020.

J. E. Beale. Llewellyn's portrait commissioned by Bournemouth Corporation. (Nigel Beale)

Beautiful casket
containing J. E. Beale's
Honorary Freeman
of the Borough scroll.
(Nigel Beale)

An active councillor, John Beale was involved in many issues of the day: plans for Pavilion, Undercliff Drive, new tramways, both West and East Overcliff Drives, etc.. His work was recognised in 1906 by a portrait, and a casket containing a scroll, making him the first local Honorary Freeman of the Borough. Yet he was also a magistrate, a helper of refugees from the First World War and one who left much of his estate to the Beales Staff Pension Fund. Was his life simply following the advice of John Wesley: 'Earn all you can, save all you can, give all you can'? After all, he had also been a travelling Wesleyan preacher in his twenties.

First Fox: Typical Early Entrepreneur

George Fox seems to indicate the nature and culture of both the Victorian times and Bournemouth's early leaders. Having spotted a good proposition in the fast-expanding town, he would take action. Builders, solicitors, banks, doctors, retailers, etc., were all needed and Fox, like others, was happy to be part of the general expansion.

He became the community stalwart who resided at and ran the Tregonwell Arms and the first post office. Having leased the Arms in 1832 from Henrietta Tregonwell,

George Fox, postmaster, who sorted mail on Tregonwell Arms bar. (Janet Burn)

he bought it outright in 1837 and later, a large adjacent area, which became the valuable Beckford estate. According to the forty-sixth Philatelic Congress of 1964, he was postmaster from 1839 to 1861, moving premises several times, including to a house on his own land at the bottom of Richmond Hill.

During his time at the Arms, Fox, a member of the Yeomanry Corps, was a well-respected general authority supplying bathing machines, stables, tea gardens, dinners and a skittle alley, as well as being postmaster, an entrepreneur, referee and property dealer!

Incidentally, two later Foxes implied by the title are the Hungry Fox, a public house in Upper Terrace Road long-since demolished, and Fox & Sons, the biggest estate agents and surveyors in Bournemouth over many years in the twentieth century.

First Pier: Built for the Paddle Steamers

Attempts were made by leading residents to finance a substantial first pier by public subscription but when these failed, the captain of the *Princess* (run by the 1848 established Weymouth paddle steamer company Cosens & Co.) suggested one could be provided more economically by a wheeled design.

No doubt he considered that such a method would be suitable for the *Princess*, which was 112 feet long and able to carry 500 passengers. The idea was to push out and retract the entire pier as supported by wheels. In the event, the new wooden pier had a retractable wheeled landing stage 6 feet by 100 feet running on rails back to a railed causeway on the beach 10 feet by 100 feet.

The project started in 1855 and the jetty opened to steamers in 1856, the date of the Bournemouth Improvement Act, which enabled a second pier of ten times the length. Although the first pier suffered storm damage before the replacement was completed by the 1856 Act's deadline of 1861, it had provided an effective service for the early town and set an excellent precedent.

First pier, often called the Jetty. Brannon engraving from 1855. (Bournemouth Library)

Founder of the Parks: From Cutting Turves to Playing Golf

In 1802, when William West (1760–1842) was living in Muscliffe by the River Stour, times were hard for the cottagers and commoners of the heath, which ran from the farms by the river to the clifftop.

Then, the Inclosure Commissioners planned to enclose the heath and ban their rights of turbary and grazing from the commons. Would they no longer be able to cut the roots of heather and gorse to dry them as turves for fuel? Despite the risk of imprisonment for workers gathering to discuss working conditions, cottagers met with this trusted and educated farmer.

He attended the Commissioners' first meeting in Ringwood with a cottagers' petition resulting in recognition of the problem in the 1805 Inclosure Award. Five areas of rather poor land, totalling 425 acres, were allocated for turf cutting (but not grazing) to eighty-six cottagers living in Pokesdown and the Stour villages from Muscliffe to Wick. However, since this right of turbary was a land use which faded out over time, the five areas were eventually made over to the council.

Thanks to William West, identified as a town founder on one of the Pavilion plaques, Bournemouth now has the great benefit of King's Park, Queen's Park, Redhill Park, Meyrick Park and Seafield Gardens for public use, albeit subject to some limitations (e.g. the golf courses at Queen's Park and Meyrick Park).

Below left: Beautiful park, Redhill Common, probably saved from development by William West.

Below right: Turf cutter Meyrick Park, 1886. Winter fuel still needed. (*Dorset Life*)

G

Ghosts at the Town Hall

When the Hotel Mont Dore opened in 1885 on a 4-acre site to offer the French Mont Dore health cure, it was considered the finest building in town. After becoming a hospital for First World War casualties, it was bought by the Corporation and from 1921 it was used as the Town Hall. According to the local paper, there have been twenty-three sightings of ghosts.

In October 2006, under the heading 'Terror at the Town Hall', the *Echo* reported ghostly goings-on including an Indian soldier with a badly tied bandage and crutch, the apparition of a nurse walking through a concrete wall and a phantom resembling a headless maharaja sitting in the mayor's chair. One employee of the council was said to have been so frightened by the resident spectres that he flung himself off the building to his death.

In November 2007, the *Echo* had some more blood-chilling tales under the heading 'Chamber of Horrors'. This time, a ghost hunter visited the building at Halloween, talking of negative energy, the date 1445, the names William, Samuel and Molly, at least two hangings and a temperature drop as you went up the stairs. During a séance, the table was tapping and rolling about.

One must make of it what one will.

Town Hall. Have there been so many ghosts that denial is impossible?

Godfrey, Sir Dan: Music Really Arrives in Bournemouth

Before the Second World War, Bournemouth was fortunate to have the sheer style of Godfrey (1868–1939), who seemed to have musical notes running through his veins. His family was very musical, including great-grandfather, grandfather, father and two uncles who were all bandmasters.

After becoming first clarinet at the Royal College of Music in 1887 and gaining a bandmaster's certificate in 1890, he toured South Africa as an opera director where he met his future wife Jessie. They married in 1892. Later, while attending an important heavyweight boxing contest where he conducted the London Military Band, he encountered Mayor Newlyn of Bournemouth, who wanted a prestige band for the town.

Godfrey began his very successful forty-one-year Bournemouth career at the Winter Gardens on Whit Monday 1893. Indeed, the Bournemouth Municipal Orchestra (Municipal changed to Symphony in 1954) was the first of its type in the country and copied by other resorts. In 1929, the orchestra moved to the newly built Pavilion; it is now based at the Poole Lighthouse. Although there were tensions with the corporation over the years, often arising from certain councillors concerned about costs, it was recognised that here was a great musical leader, producing excellent programmes.

Sir Dan Godfrey (knighted in 1922 for outstanding service to British music) was noted for supporting British composers, who often conducted their own compositions, for producing a high-quality musical experience and for wisely mixing popular with classical. His approach thus appealed to all tastes and ensured good audiences who could also watch variety acts in between the musical performances and were even allowed to choose and participate in some of it. No wonder he was well liked.

Dan Godfrey and Bournemouth Municipal Orchestra in Winter Gardens. (Alwyn Ladell)

Golden Sands

The 7 miles of sands are arguably Bournemouth's biggest attraction, the long expanse of gently shelving beach being ideal for bathing. Furthermore, the open outlook gives a sense of enclosure, being in a U-shaped setting with the Isle of Wight to the east and the Isle of Purbeck to the west. There is not another south coast resort with such a shoreline and viewpoint.

After the sea broke through the chalk ridge joining The Needles to Old Harry Rocks about 10,000 years ago, Poole Bay was gradually formed by the action of the tides and scouring currents transporting the sands to the east. It has proved difficult to control ongoing coastal erosion purely by groynes and sea walls, whose purpose is to save the cliffs and consequently the roads and properties above them. For example, stormy seas can undercut a wall and cause the promenade behind to collapse.

After it was realised that proper sea defence requires regular sediment replenishment to the beaches, they were considerably widened and deepened over time, now almost reaching the level of the promenades.

Thus, despite the inclusion of some sharp shingle within the replenishment, particularly where the erosion risk is greatest towards Hengistbury Head, and also some very sandy promenades on occasion, the tourism department should always be able to promote Bournemouth and its golden sands.

Idyllic sandy scene from Boscombe clifftop to the Purbecks.

Bay from
Durley Chine.
P. L. M. Ward.
(Mrs Myrna
Chave and
RCAGM)

Granville, Doctor, in 1841: Expert Advice for the Village of Bourne

Although Tregonwell's grave inscription says that he founded the town as a watering place in 1810, neither he nor the main landowner, Tapps, wanted much development. However, when Tapps died in 1835, his son, Sir George William Tapps-Gervis, took a totally different view. By 1838 he had achieved the building of Westover Villas, the Belle Vue Boarding House and the Bath Hotel, which opened on 28 June, the coronation day of Queen Victoria.

In 1841, Tapps-Gervis invited Granville (1783–1872) to visit Bourne. As the respected author of the *Spas of England*, he was greatly impressed and added a chapter about the village to his influential book. He stressed the importance of the relatively high winter temperature, as verified by measurements taken for him and the evident need to guide development. Dwellings were required for both wealthy invalids and other residents. Granville, enjoying his visit, took a wide view of everything, even proposing that the servants living on the top floor of the Bath Hotel be rehoused in outbuildings and the top floor be rebuilt to give a better ceiling height for guests. Other recommendations were that Poole Bay should be renamed Bourne Bay and that a cove be formed for pleasure boats where the Brook met the sea.

He strongly opposed 'bricks and mortar speculators' building without restriction because that would ruin the town for the invalids. He wanted a spacious town, a 'unique Montpellier' rather than a huddled, noisy, vulgar and bustling sea-watering place. To ensure good attendances for a new church, he particularly wanted it sited on low ground near the centre, not high on the East Cliff as suggested by Ferrey. Widow Henrietta Tregonwell should be respectfully approached for part of her substantial ownership between Wimborne Road and Old Christchurch Road. In the event, St Peter's was built nearby on Tapps-Gervis land but sadly, Sir George died the year before its completion in 1843.

Otherwise, Granville praised the dry and permeable sandy soil as beneficial for invalids but disliked the 'prairie' land by the Brook with its coarse grass and miserable sheep, instead recommending a promenade garden leading to a new pier and facilities for pleasure boats. Staying in one of the Westover Road Villas, he said its well gave him good soft water and even had the Brook tested, finding it to be the same and clear of any dung contamination. Indeed, he scotched the rumour that a first drink taken from the Brook would lead to relaxation of the bowels.

In short, Granville maintained that 1841 Bourne was uniquely suited for developing as a health resort but that would have to be done in the right way to succeed. Much of his advice was heeded.

Doctor Augustus Bozzi Granville by Alexander Craig. (Wellcome Collection, CCbySA 4.0)

Gulliver, Isaac: Gentleman of the Night

Perhaps controversially, Gulliver (1745–1822) has a plaque at the Pavilion among other founders of Bournemouth in recognition of his large and successful contraband operation based in Kinson, followed by a career as a legitimate wine merchant. Since many from all classes were involved in and supported the Free Trade, 'Old Gulliver' was regarded as a champion of local industry. His smugglers, with their powdered hair, were known as 'White Wigs'.

Although a major player employing many men and ships, in a sometimes vicious occupation, it was his proud boast that he had never killed a man. His horses and waggons delivered to London, the Midlands and Bristol.

There are stories of hiding places and underground tunnelling at Gulliver's house and rope marks in the stones of St Andrew's Church, Kinson, caused by hauling the contraband up the church tower. On one occasion when the revenue men had a search warrant for him, he reputedly escaped arrest by playing dead in a coffin while his wife cried over it.

He may have obtained the king's pardon for smugglers in 1782, but an 1867 report describes his last huge landing at Bourne Valley in 1800, a time when Captain Tregonwell of the Dorset Volunteer Rangers was tasked with fighting smuggling. Gulliver amassed considerable property, served as a churchwarden for Wimborne Minster and died a wealthy and widely respected man.

H. P. Parker painting hung in Tregonwell Arms, central character Isaac Gulliver. (Bournemouth Library)

H

Halifax Bomber Crash: Wartime Tragedy at Wimborne Road

It is distressing when any town suffers the horror of air raids, but there is something particularly sad about loss of life involving a British aircraft on home soil.

On 21 March 1944, the twenty-year-old RAF pilot Sgt Denis R. Evans took off from Hurn Airport in a Handley Page Halifax Mark II bound for North Africa. It is estimated that the heavily loaded bomber was in the air for about 10 miles and three minutes before the crash that caused the death of himself, six other crew members and two civilians.

During that time, it is believed that the direction of travel changed from south to north, a port engine failed and the tail plane did not perform as it should due to a design fault; control was inevitably lost. As the aircraft hit the ground behind a block of apartments, there was devastation and a huge ball of flame. In the illustration, the

Last moments of doomed Halifax bomber. (Moordown Halifax Memorial)

aircraft image is superimposed on a post-crash photograph of the site (i.e. showing a supposed pre-crash, upside down orientation and position).

Following some detailed research that has cleared the pilot from any blame, the Moordown Halifax Memorial was installed in 2011 near to the site of the accident. Despite the unveiling being so distant in time, the recognition of what happened was greatly appreciated by relatives of those killed.

Health and Pleasure: Created by Bournemouth's Magic Kettle

After its initial status as a playground for the aristocracy in the early nineteenth century, Bournemouth became a top health resort for rich Victorians who liked its climate, the scent of the pines and health facilities. Probably the biggest facility was the Mont Dore Hotel, built in 1885, with its varied system of baths and choice of twenty different modes of using the water externally. The demand for such a specialist hotel was much less by the time it was taken over by the council in 1921 for use as the Town Hall.

However, a cartoon from 1904 shows that it was then judged necessary to satirise the whole notion of the town's healthy air. It followed Sir James Crichton-Browne (1840–1938) famously extolling 'the wonderful health-giving properties of Bournemouth's air'. He puts Pure Air into the Magic Kettle, which heats it with Bournemouth Breezes. Mayor John Elmes Beale then pours it into a steaming mug, giving clouds of Health and Pleasure to all.

Perhaps we should not laugh at the eminent doctor's opinion as ridiculed here in the *Bournemouth Graphic*. After all, he did live to be ninety-seven years old!

'Health secret' of Bournemouth's success.

Hengistbury Head

This attractive eastern extremity of Bournemouth was purchased before auction by the council in 1930 from its owner, Harry Gordon Selfridge. The price was £25,250 and area covered 422 acres. His grandiose plans for major development including two castles had come to nothing for financial reasons.

From before 1759 until at least 1836, the top of the headland sported a major building some 45 feet high known as Warren Summerhouse, which was used for leisure, a lookout and as a landmark for shipping.

Today, Hengistbury Head, a Local Nature Reserve and SSSI, is a prime tourist destination enjoyed by an estimated 1 million visitors every year. Its international importance for archaeology and geology is publicly recognised by the excellent visitor centre.

Above: Eastern view of Hengistbury Head, The Needles and the Island's White Bear.

Right: Warren Summerhouse, Hengistbury. 360 degree viewing platform. (Christopher Hollick)

Hyacinth and Tchaikovsky: Alligator at the Winter Gardens

Music lovers enjoying a Bournemouth Symphony Orchestra concert in April 1956 were blissfully unaware that stretched out among them was an alligator.

Hyacinth was not noticed because she was only a year old, 15 inches long and nestled under a scarf in the lap of nineteen-year-old Elisabeth Staddon. She seemed to beat time with her tail, but since no one had told her when not to applaud, she gave a few little honks after the second movement of Tchaikovsky's *Fifth Symphony* drew to its fairly quiet close.

The alligator belonged to journalist Hugh Noyes, who worked with Elisabeth at a newspaper office in Devizes, Wiltshire. Driving back after a weekend at home in Ventnor, Isle of Wight, he had arranged to give her a lift from her home in Christchurch.

When they stopped off at Bournemouth's Winter Gardens to catch the BSO's Sunday evening concert, Hugh was reluctant to leave Hyacinth in a tank in the back of his car, so she went along too. Elisabeth's friend, *Bournemouth Times* reporter Ian Stevenson, sat on one side of her and Hugh on the other to help ensure that Hyacinth was not noticed. And Ian coughed to cover her honks.

After the concert, Hyacinth caused a stir by making a public appearance at the crowded El Cabala coffee bar in Old Christchurch Road. Sadly for her, the menu did not include her favourite dishes of mice, horsemeat and cod liver oil!

This baby alligator is probably larger than the Tchaikovsky attendee. (Pixabay licence)

I

Iford's Old Bridge

Before the first Tuckton Bridge was built in 1883, the ancient village of Iford was the lowest road crossing point of the River Stour.

The name Iford may derive from 'eye' (island) or 'ea' (shallow) and 'ford', probably because the river could be crossed here by a ford or bridge in sections. Currently, there is a bridge over the main river, then a short road over an island and finally another bridge over a minor branch of the river and low ground on the Christchurch side.

Two sixteenth-century wills held at Holdenhurst Church left money for 'Iver Bridge', which was so named on Saxton's Hampshire map of 1575 and referred to in Leland's Itinerary Vol. 1 (1535 to 1543) as Iver Bridge of Stone, 2 miles from Christchurch. Yet the existing Grade II listed Old Iford Bridge only dates from the seventeenth to the nineteenth century. The nearest two arches, of the main section seen from the village, were built in 1784.

Since the bridge had become completely inadequate by 1930, it was replaced upstream for vehicular traffic and retained for pedestrians only. No doubt many were relieved; no more angry altercations between motorists who met in the centre and both claimed priority.

Main attractive span of the old bridge viewed from Iford.

Long, narrow structure meant regular disputes when vehicles met head to head.

Iford Village of Old: Recollections from Frederick Barnes' Childhood up to the 1920s

The lifestyle and crafts of this bygone age are now truly lost.

How much do we know today of brightly painted farm waggons and skilfully made hay ricks, smithy and wheelwright (hand tools only), hand milking and thatching, mud-walled buildings and that difficult River Stour crossing on the old bridge?

Timber, coal and gravel were supplied; waggon wheels were fitted with iron tyres; one busy villager ran a mini zoo, tea gardens, the village shop and a boat hire business. Steam engines did threshing and traction; pigs were killed to provide pork for all; children played in the river; strong horses were prized for farming duties; everyone knew everyone; there were home births and old folks stayed at home. Moose Hall was built and used for recreation and the Iford Brass Band.

Iford also boasted the New Inn, an engineering company, an undertaker, owls and bats. In such an agricultural world, people were familiar not only with culling rats and rabbits but also helping each other out. Village bliss ... or was it?

Iford Village.
Postcard from
'Flo', dated 8
December 1905.
(Alwyn Ladell)

Iford Village, near Bournemouth. Yours very sincerely Flo 8 th[?]

Inclosure and Napoleon: War with France Enabled Bournemouth

Before Nelson's victory at Trafalgar in 1805, common land was of limited agricultural potential due to commoners' rights. The government therefore decided to sell off the commons to make the country more self-sufficient by improving productivity.

Under the Christchurch Inclosure Act 1802 and the Award of West Stour in 1805, the area was divided into parcels for sale. One applicant in particular, Sir George Ivison Tapps, secured a huge amount of what is now prime land. However, Bourne Heath was mainly too poor for arable or pasture, which led to the planting of thousands of pine trees by the new freeholders. Many commoners were partially compensated by the allocation of five areas to cut turf for fuel. However, now called Redhill Park, Seafield Gardens, King's Park, Meyrick Park and Queen's Park, they have long since been taken over by the council for public recreation.

Since commoners' rights were mainly extinguished, Tapps was not only able to plant woodlands, but also to begin selling off sections to Lewis Tregonwell, who greatly limited building on his new estate, known as Bourne Tregonwell, in his lifetime. However, development of Bourne began in earnest after inheritance by the two sons of Tapps and Tregonwell.

So it is that a national policy, of agricultural improvement in time of war, provided in Bournemouth a foundation for property development, one which eventually created a highly successful seaside resort, as enhanced by attractive parks and the town's famous pines.

Joseph Cutler: Builder, Campaigner and Enthusiast

Bournemouth's fast growth in Victorian times depended on the insight and sheer hard work of people like Joseph Cutler (1830–1910), who played a large part in public service and building development.

The son of a Christchurch fisherman, Cutler was apprenticed to a plumber, joined the Australian gold rush, settled in Bournemouth as a house builder, was declared bankrupt in 1869, but went on to become a controversial town celebrity. He was a spirited and cheerful man with firm views and the enthusiasm to push through building schemes. For example, before the West Cliff Zig Zag, he constructed Joseph's Steps from salvaged pier timbers washed ashore after a storm. He was also a volunteer fireman, first rowing club captain, Bournemouth Commissioner and later councillor, Burial Board member, Sunday school worker and campaigner for women's rights.

Joseph contributed suggestions about the pier, the Pavilion and the need for drainage plans. One letter in 1871 says that bylaws should be amended to prevent people keeping pigs in Richmond Hill and Poole Road to stop their 'great effluvia'. But his letters were not always published as his views were sometimes deemed too opinionated.

Joseph Cutler immortalised in green tiles at 1877 shops, Joseph's Terrace, Bournemouth.

Despite some unpopularity, Joseph was never fazed, presenting the town with both cemetery trees and his autobiography. In 1881, he even sent 35 lbs of strawberries to the inmates of the Christchurch Workhouse because the Guardians had eaten the ones grown within the grounds. He remarked in a P.S. 'The poor ye have always with you'.

Joy's Folly: The Beautiful Church Glen Lost Forever

Carpenter Henry Joy (1822–1906) proved himself to be a shrewd builder, though his arcade development was christened Joy's Folly.

The arcade site was Church Glen, a ravine crossed by a rustic bridge (installed in 1853, had a toll of a halfpenny) adorned by ivy and wild roses. Below the bridge, gardens were laid out beside a tributary of the Bourne running from The Lansdowne. Church Glen being so attractive, Joy's arcade scheme of 1866 was criticised for ruining a well-loved beauty spot.

A further negative opinion was that the twenty-three shops, with two floors of residential accommodation above and basements below, would not find tenants. Aside from the criticism, he had to grapple with foundation and financial difficulties.

Yet Joy understood the commercial merit of the location between Gervis Place and Old Christchurch Road. While the units were initially slow to let, they became fully successful after the glazed barrel roof was added in 1872, providing all-weather shopping with plenty of natural light. In 1884, he went on to build the Westbourne Arcade.

Employing a mixture of enterprise, hard work and resilience, Henry Joy eventually triumphed with the arcade scheme, which is now a Grade II listed building. No longer dubbed Joy's Folly, which is now a Grade II listed building and an asset to the town.

No longer dubbed Joy's Folly, The Arcade is a valuable shopping destination.

Ken Baily, Town Mascot: Bournemouth's Most Irrepressible Resident!

Ken Baily (1911–93), Freeman of Bournemouth and Royalist, personified the cheerful side of the town through his endless brightly coloured photo opportunities. He always seemed to be there.

Ken frequently dressed as John Bull, swam in the sea on Christmas Day as a member of the Spartans, ran between the piers every year with a flaming torch to start the fireworks and raised the spirits of all he met, many of whom, like the author, had their hands most firmly shaken. Although he was both self-appointed and a member of committees, the distinction rarely mattered. Either way, he was regularly in the *Echo* due to his attending so many events in those eye-catching outfits.

As a local charity worker, committee member for both the Regatta and Athletic Club, newspaper columnist, wearer of a red-tail coat and provider of tapers to visitors for them to light the town's summer illuminations, one might have thought that was enough. But his efforts went well beyond his adopted town to include the whole country and, indeed, the world. For example, Australia. 'What are you doing here?' asked the Queen on spotting Ken among a crowd in a Sydney street. 'I'd go anywhere for you, Ma'am', replied Baily. He was England's unofficial sporting cheerleader at Twickenham in 1982 when Erica Roe streaked on the rugby field. She said later that she was soon 'shrouded by that ridiculous man in his flag'. That was Ken.

Opposite: Ebullient Ken Baily adding atmosphere to the 1989 Westbourne Carnival. (Alwyn Ladell)

Lower Gardens: Perfect Link Between Sea and Town Centre

The town is lucky to have the Bourne Stream and Gardens, placed as they are on very valuable real estate. In the early days, they were used for grazing after their reclaim from marshy land. Dr Granville's strong 1841 advice for conversion from pasture to ornamental gardens was perhaps decisive.

But whether they are here by luck or judgement does not matter in that commercial redevelopment in the future is now unthinkable. Although the Middle and Upper Gardens are important, the Lower Gardens are the busiest, providing a wide and ornamental pedestrianised link from the sea to The Square with all its town centre facilities. Visitors frequently marvel at how the tiny Bourne Stream could possibly give its name to such a major town.

In summer, there are magical Candlelight Procession evenings for children who get free tapers to light candles from the gardens to the pier. The generous amount of comfortable seating, the aviary, the minigolf, the winter ice skating, the art exhibitions, the summer bandstand concerts and, most of all, the large publicly accessible areas of grass and meticulously maintained flowerbeds add up to something special.

Bournemouth's Lower Gardens viewed along the Bourne Stream towards The Square.

Mansion to Royal Exeter

A special mention is needed for an imposing early residence in what is now central Bournemouth; before Mrs Henrietta Tregonwell, few thought to have a substantial summer retreat in this idyllic spot. That said, there is no evidence that her motivation ever encompassed the idea of a resort.

Occupied in 1812, the Mansion, having six or seven bedrooms, was located on high ground for the best possible outlook over the shallow valley, sea and Needles. Sometimes, it was rented to others including the Marchioness of Exeter in 1820, so creating new names, Exeter House and Exeter Road. The 'Royal' was added after a ten-day visit by the Empress of Austria in 1888.

Although today's Royal Exeter Hotel is a greatly extended building, the original gabled front wall can still be identified, albeit the façade's two original side gables have been rebuilt at a higher level.

Royal Exeter Hotel was part of the 1910 Bournemouth Centenary celebrations. (Alwyn Ladell)

N

Naming of the Town

There is a simple origin for the name, based on people noting the rather unusual feature of a small stream emerging from a wide, shallow valley in the cliffs. The old word for stream being 'burna' and for mouth, 'muth', the purpose of the name was self-explanatory: the mouth of a stream at the coast.

The earliest reference is probably in a Christchurch Cartulary Memorandum of 13 October 1406 about a wreck on the Westover estate near 'la Bournemowthe'. The 'wreck' was an eighteen-foot great fish, which was taken to Wick and there cut up into forty pieces.

A defence map from 1539, produced for Henry VIII, has Bowurnemothe and the Saxton map of 1575 Burnemouthe. But in 1759, Isaac Taylor's map refers to Bourne Chine. More recently, the Ordnance Survey map of 1810 gives Bourne Mouth, which compares with the Marine Village of Bourne as described by Ferrey in his plans from 1836. Yet Mrs Drax Grosvenor clearly named it Bournemouth in 1816 as per the illustration with 'Peep into Futurity'.

By the time of the Bournemouth Improvement Act 1856, the present name of the town was firmly established.

National Sanatorium: Victorian Charity in Action

Tuberculosis thrived from around 1800, when many lived in cramped conditions on poor diets, and consumptives were rarely hospitalised due to the low chance of cure. When the risk of infection was finally appreciated by 1900, isolation was used but treatment was mainly limited to convalescence until streptomycin became available after its discovery in 1943.

Having decided on a south coast sanatorium for the recuperation of patients, London's Brompton Hospital chose the embryo health resort of Bournemouth for its dryness, equability and mildness of temperature. A prominent 3-acre south facing site was chosen. Prince Albert laid the foundation stone and Charles Dickens was among the many supporters. Built in 1855 with forty beds, the Sanatorium was given a satisfactory report for its first six months' operation and by 1856, it was financially independent of the hospital. Clearly, it was an era of action, not bureaucracy.

Although royal patronage from Queen Victoria was achieved in 1869 and many of 'the great and the good' offered help, the Sanatorium's finances were never easy.

An extension was built in 1863 and in 1866 a chapel, dedicated to St Luke the Physician, attendance by patients being compulsory. A new wing followed in 1873. By 1887, the chapel was being made available to the invalids at the adjoining Hotel Mont Dore (built in 1885, now the Town Hall) and the hotel's baths for the TB patients in return. However, there was conflict in 1900 when the Sanatorium's new open air treatment resulted in the patients' coughing, disturbing the hotel's invalids. Once streptomycin became available, TB was controlled and the premises were closed in 1990 with the opening of the new Bournemouth Hospital.

After years of disuse, the buildings were altered and new ones added to provide a secluded retirement home of character: Brompton Court.

National Sanatorium. Engraving from 1855 when building was complete. (Alwyn Ladell)

Now Brompton Court, the site is screened by trees from road and gardens.

O

One-mile 'Circular' Boundary: First Official Bournemouth

Once Westover Villas and the first two hotels were built by 1838, the potential for fast growth was clear. Increasingly, attention was drawn to the need for effective administration of the village as shown by the population figures: 695 in 1851, 1,707 in 1861 and 5,896 in 1871.

To tackle this and also the desire for a pier, the Bournemouth Improvement Act was passed in 1856 and Commissioners appointed. The area's central point was the front door of the Belle Vue Hotel, formerly called the Belle Vue Boarding House, located where the Pavilion now stands. Using a radius of 1 mile, the circle was mapped so that the land within it would become subject to the Commissioners' powers, an innovation so effective that borough status was not needed until 1890. Although the area was largely uninhabited, today's main road layout can be seen on Creeke's 1857 map.

Powers were granted for roads, drainage, refuse disposal, the holding of markets and the new pier, as financed by a general rate. The lord of the manor and John Tregonwell (son of Lewis) were among the Commissioners named in the Act, which also laid down provisions for future elections by ratepayers.

By incorporating other legislation, many detailed powers could be exercised, e.g. under S.42 of the Towns Improvement Clauses Act 1847, householders could be compelled to provide privies with ash pits.

The Commissioners could acquire land, borrow money and collect pier tolls. The Act set out maximum tolls for over 200 types of goods, which might be laded or unladed at the future pier including fox (five shillings), barrel of anchovies (three pennies), score of hogs (three shillings), ton of flint stones (three pennies) and harpsichord (four shillings). It was indeed a different world.

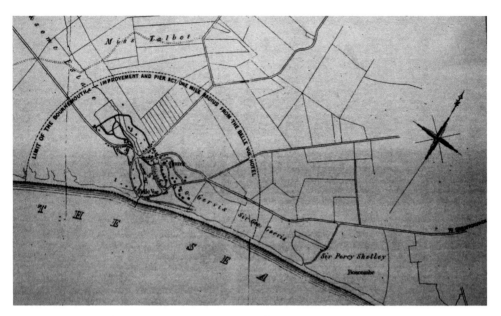

C. C. Creeke's 1857 'Circular Bournemouth' map of the village. (Bournemouth Library)

P

Paradise, Wild Garden by The Square

The council deserves great credit for carefully maintaining the formal gardens at a high standard despite the loss of about 75 per cent of their maintenance staff over the years. But this area, known as 'Paradise' at the southern end of the Central Gardens, is very different having been kept rather wild on purpose.

Within what seems to be a somewhat historic and overgrown small meadow, it can be seen that the Bourne Stream has a quaint undisturbed island, which might never have survived had this been part of the public gardens.

As shown by the six-bar metal gate being locked, there is no official public access, which would most probably damage this unique backwater, 'unique' because although it literally adjoins the northern side of The Square, it is easy to miss in the rush of today. When you walk all around the site from The Square to the ornamental bridge on the other side, there is great contrast between the natural peace of Paradise and the backdrop of the busy town, including for example the Town Hall.

Here is a surprising window into the past, blessing the observer with a real sense of tranquillity.

'Paradise' – peace and calm alongside The Square.

Pavilion of 1929: Nearly a Century in the Making

After inheriting land from his father, who died in 1835, Sir George Tapps-Gervis (1795–1842) was keen to promote development. Although his architect, Benjamin Ferrey, visualised an ornamental Pleasure Gardens Pagoda at the site of the present Pavilion, it was a rather upmarket scheme when Bourne was still a tiny and little-known village.

In practice, the Belle Vue Boarding House was erected in 1838 to supply relatively economical accommodation, its adjoining Assembly Rooms becoming popular for many uses including worship, public meetings, dances and concerts. Clearly, this was felt by Sir George to be more appropriate than the pagoda at that time, yet a worthy forerunner of the Pavilion.

In 1873, land was made over to the Commissioners by the Gervis family for public gardens and buildings, the idea of a pavilion being strongly promoted from 1876. Many years of controversy followed until the competition-winning design of G. Wyville Home and Shirley Knight was chosen and the foundation stone laid in 1925.

Listed in 1998 and described as a multi-purpose entertainment venue for a major seaside resort, many now worry about the Pavilion's possible loss through unsatisfactory redevelopment.

Pagoda with a waterwheel in the Brook. Ferrey's View of Bournemouth. (RCAGM)

Pavilion. A triumph of design making excellent use of this prime location.

Peep Into Futurity: Satirical Play by Mrs Sarah Frances Erle Drax Grosvenor

When this play was written in 1816, the Drax Grosvenors occupied Cliff Cottage on the other side of the road from Tregonwell's Mansion of 1812.

Sarah included in her play an illustration of the sea view in 1816 (upper picture) and her 1876 forecast (lower picture). The first showed merely two buildings and two bathing machines.

The 1876 numbered features can all be just about identified except for nine but we can see that must be the church (upper right):

1. New hotel on Paradise Row kept by Miss Becky Russell.
2. Opposition Row with the hotel kept by Mr James Payne.
3. The Market Place.
4. Windmill Castle, the residence of Sir Isaac and Lady Cherubina de Tapps.

Bournemouth in 1816 and as then imagined in 1876. (Mrs Julia Smith)

5. The Assembly Rooms and Bazaar kept by the Miss Paynes, with the Coffee House.
6. The Royal Tea Gardens.
7. The new bridge over the River Bourne, by the voluntary subscriptions of the fashionable residents of this frequented and distinguished bathing place.
8. The Theatre Royal (manager and scene-shifter Mr Canterell, once an upholsterer, Blandford).
9. The new church on Meg's Hill (organist Sam Ricketts. Master of the Ceremonies Mr. H. Hayter).
10. The gaol.
11. The Boarding School for Young Ladies, overlooking the Royal Tea Gardens, kept by Amelia Blacklock.

Although the play is mainly concerned with poking fun at the inhabitants of 1816 by imagining the affairs of sixty years later, the lower picture provides an intriguing prophecy of the future health resort.

Pier

The pier area has always been the town's natural leisure focus. The beach, the Bourne Stream and the Gardens are easily approached by a level walk from The Square or on a reasonable slope from the East Cliff and the West Cliff, and always with the benefit of the excellent emerging sea view.

A major reason for the 1856 Bournemouth Improvement Act was to enable the construction of a good pier. Over time, nearby facilities have included bathing machines, reading room, public baths, the Pier Hotel (replaced by Pavilion), other hotels, Pier Approach Baths (replaced by IMAX cinema and then by open air leisure venue), Oceanarium and the Bournemouth International Centre. As a Director of Tourism might say: 'It makes Bournemouth unique!'

West Cliff outlook, perhaps shortly after 1876 storm. (Janet Burn)

The days of regattas and rowing boats on the beach.

In 1877, Willie West performed three times daily. (Janet Burn)

Charabanc, 1921, with a possibly hostile driver at Sydenham's shop. (Alwyn Ladell)

Bournemouth
Pier today.

East Cliff outlook,
pier approach as
modernised and
commercialised.

Pinecliffe Avenue, Southbourne:
A Fifties Childhood

When my parents moved to this road from Essex with their harsh memories of the Blitz, the idea of a four-bedroomed guest house was most appealing. Like most, we had no family car in 1948, but the clifftop and shops were close and the trolley buses at Fisherman's Walk were popular and efficient.

The twenty-year old, well-built, spacious house was freezing in winter. Domestic central heating was unheard of at the time but we dressed quickly and the kitchen was kept warm overnight by the Ideal solid fuel boiler.

Familiar view of Pinecliffe Avenue from the clifftop.

Neighbours packed our lounge to see the coronation in 1953 on one of the few TVs in the area. The official Town Guide for 1954 gave the summer rates for our guest house: from 5.5 to 6.5 guineas per week, full board. One important thing was having an old bike (no gears) to roam the town, followed by the huge excitement of a new one (with three gears) in 1958, allowing much greater distances. There were no crash helmets or Lycra outfits, just my mother calling out from the back door: 'Be careful on the roads!'

The guest house was very hard work and I fear my contribution was getting under my parents' feet. On long summer days, they were happy to see my brother Peter and me taking sandwiches to the private beach just past the Southbourne promenade. An attraction for the guests was our beach hut located below the cliff at the sea end of Pinecliffe Avenue. Naturally, Peter and I often scorned Gordon's Zig Zag and reached the hut by climbing up and down that cliff, cuts and bruises being a normal part of life.

Portman Lodge to BH2

Built around 1810, this four-roomed dwelling, in its spacious grounds, was first called Symes' Cottage after Lewis Tregonwell's butler. Later, it was greatly extended or rebuilt to provide fourteen rooms. Was it erected before the Mansion, which was to be Lewis and Henrietta's summer residence, first occupied in 1812? The answer: is probably yes, with Symes supervising the building of that residence from his cottage.

Following Lewis's death in 1832, Henrietta lived in the cottage, which became known as Portman Lodge after her maiden name. From here, she could see across Exeter

Road to her husband's cenotaph, a huge urn on a pedestal in Cranborne Gardens. In 1846, she arranged for the bodies of Lewis and her infant son Grosvenor to be exhumed from Anderson and reburied at St Peter's Church. She died herself later that year, joining him in the family vault.

In June 1922, when the occupiers were Mr Walters of Rebbecks and Newmans wine merchants, there was a serious and baffling fire. Initially, hose and hatchet was applied to the front thatch. But it smouldered and spread out of sight below the surface of the roof, creating thick smoke and fanned by a north wind. Although four hoses were used on three great volumes of smoke each with small flames, jets of fire soon appeared at the south window.

Crowds gathered. Many helped to remove furniture including some beautiful suites and a grand piano. Later, at considerable risk, another piano was taken out together with much of the upstairs contents. A wall leaned, bulged and crashed, almost injuring two firemen using a ladder against it.

A rebuild was reportedly done, but that was replaced in 1931 by the Bournemouth Bus and Coach Station, itself destroyed by fire in 1976. After many years as an open NCP car park, the site was fully redeveloped by February 2017 as the large BH2 entertainment complex.

The Second House built in **Bournemouth.**

Built by Squire Tregonwell about 1810. Called Tregonwell House. Name Altered to Portman Lodge When it was occupied by Lord Portman.

Dubiously annotated postcard of Portman Lodge, 1913. (Alwyn Ladell)

Queen's Park

Named after Queen Alexandra of Denmark in 1902, this terrain has broadly evolved from providing fuel for the poor in 1805 to becoming an excellent golf course.

For centuries, cottagers had rights to cut turf for fuel and were unhappy when these turbary rights were to be extinguished under the 1802 Christchurch Inclosure Act. Their appeal to the Commissioners, for ongoing turbary allocations, was successful, common 60 of 136 acres (now most of Queen's Park) being one of five areas so identified. However, after Sir George Ivison Tapps' 1805 purchase subject to turbary rights, that need declined while the wish for public open space increased.

Queen's Park Golf Course, once a common providing turf for fuel.

Under the Bournemouth Corporation Act 1900, Tapps' heir sold the land to the council in trust for public use, requiring it to be 'forever open and unbuilt'. Now that turbary had ended and practical management was needed for such a major open area in a thriving town, the council decreed a golf course and pavilion, which opened in 1905.

The Act allowed not only for roads, trees and lodges for keepers, but also for the council to provide facilities for health, recreation and enjoyment. Inevitably, several controversies followed, e.g. Sunday golf, axing trees, fencing, managing the big pond, conflict between golfers and walkers, permissibility of disposal for tennis courts, etc. Non-golf uses have included band performances, rifle range, horse riding, drilling of troops in the First World War and annual community events.

The Queen's Park Improvement and Protection Society has helped the council to shape policy relating to effective public access. For example, 1965 plans for tennis courts, bowling greens and a pavilion were rejected at a public enquiry. Recognising that the golf course already inhibited public use and enjoyment, the minister determined that the council had no right to dispose of any part of this public open space.

Signage shows that Queen's Park is fully open to public access including two suggested walks of 2 km and 3 km. There is also the cheerful 1983 Woodpecker Café, a first floor bar and restaurant, built above the 1967 replacement of the original pavilion lost to the Wessex Way. Separately, the charity BH Live operate a gym and swimming pool on the southern edge of the park.

In essence, while some consider that the golf course conflicts with the 1900 Act and its true purpose of unrestricted public open space, others see it as today's best land management.

R

Railway Must Be Hidden

The Commissioners worried about a good connection to London in the same way that they were reluctant later to have trams. Would the town's elegance be lost? Yet the commercial imperative won the day in both cases albeit with compromises. The railway was kept out of the centre and relegated to cuttings where possible, while the trams were designed to run without overhead wires in the town centre.

By 1872, the service was still poor, the few trains to London from Bournemouth East station taking about four hours via a slow line through Ringwood. But LSWR's plan for a terminus close to the Mont Dore Hotel, St Stephen's Church and the National Sanatorium was refused as injurious to the health resort. Instead, the inadequate Bournemouth East was replaced on the other side of Holdenhurst Road by a much better one, today's Bournemouth Station. Having ensured an out-of-town location for the town's main station, the line west to Poole was also placed further away from the centre than first planned and mainly in cuttings.

It had all been very difficult. A planned line to West Moors was dropped; the Didcot, Newbury and Southampton Railway unsuccessfully suggested a connection from a new Bournemouth station at Dean Park Road to Southampton, then using the company's and GWR lines to Paddington via Didcot; the Commissioners wanted to prevent a monopoly by having two competing lines to London.

In April 1883, they approved LSWR's modified scheme, which included an extension from Brockenhurst to Christchurch. It was faster, more direct, quicker to implement and affected merely heathland not forest as needed by the Didcot scheme. The ceremonial opening was in March 1888.

Bournemouth got its fast link to London while minimising disturbance, an outcome respecting the following quote from the Bournemouth Visitor's Directory:

> Tis well from far to hear the railway scream;
> And watch the curling lingering clouds of steam;
> But let not Bournemouth-health's approved abode
> Court the near presence of the Iron road.

Rattenbury Murder

In March 1935, the retired, prominent British architect Francis Rattenbury, aged sixty-seven, was viciously attacked with a mallet causing a severe head wound from which he died in hospital four days later. The scene of the crime was the living room of his house in Manor Road on the East Cliff and the cause was a lover's jealousy.

The Old Bailey trial that followed has been described as the sensation of 1935, involving as it did a public petition signed by over 300,000 pleading for mercy for the killer.

Since November 1934 after some marital difficulties partly caused by Rattenbury's bouts of depression, his much younger wife, Alma, an outstanding musician, had been having an affair. It seems that she seduced the couple's chauffeur George Stoner, aged eighteen, a young man who later turned out to be violent and threatened to commit suicide.

They were both charged with murder, Stoner being sentenced to hang while Alma was found innocent and released. She was grief-stricken within days, committing suicide by stabbing herself and then drowning in a tributary of the River Avon at Three Arches railway bridge, Christchurch. On appeal, Stoner's sentence was commuted to lifetime penal servitude.

Following release in 1942, he joined the Army and fought in the Second World War, living until March 2000 and dying in Christchurch Hospital on the sixty-fifth anniversary of the murder and close to the location of Alma's suicide.

Terence Rattigan's successful play, *Cause Célèbre*, was based on these tragic events.

Reindeer Camp to Long Groyne

Some 12,500 years ago, a reindeer camp on Hengistbury Head overlooked a shallow green valley across the River Solent to a high chalk ridge running from what is now The Needles to Old Harry. Late Stone Age hunters would drive migrating wild horses and reindeer down the slope and into the river for the kill.

As the inter-glacial period progressed, sea level naturally rose swiftly by some 400 feet leading to the destruction of the ridge and the formation of Poole Bay, the view being transformed to a sea horizon. Current sea level rise is about six inches per century. The Head is an erosion remnant, which partly survived the bay formation because its ironstones enabled it to provide an effective eastern headland.

Sadly, the defensive apron of these rocks, at the Head's base, was removed for smelting in the nineteenth century by coal merchant, councillor and architect J. Holloway of Christchurch, so allowing the coastal erosion of Bournemouth's soft sedimentary cliffs to proceed apace. Something had to be done to hold back the scouring action of the sea. In 1938, the council finally replaced the ironstones with Long Groyne, which has since been rock-armoured and reinforced. However, due to some continuing clifftop erosion, archaeologists did a rescue excavation of the residue of the old campsite, the latest work being completed in 1983 with the recovery of thousands of flints.

Long Groyne strengthened in 2019. Black plastic (bottom left) marks the 1983 rescue excavation site.

This land at Bournemouth's eastern edge has thus changed from a very cold inland Stone Age campsite seasonally occupied by hunters to a viewing point above sea defence works needed to protect the Head and the town.

Rolls, The Hon. Charles Stewart

The co-founder of Rolls-Royce Ltd, who was born in 1877, had a short and tragic connection with Bournemouth, arriving in July for the one-week 1910 International Aviation Meeting and having a fatal air crash on its second day. Before the Meeting began, Rolls had installed an unofficial and ultimately fatal modification to the tail of his Wright Flyer. Although he won the competition for the slowest circuit, which was very difficult due to the risk of stalling, the prize had to be awarded posthumously.

The night before the accident on 12 July, Rolls was dining with the rich and famous Lady Abdy, who wanted him to take her for a flight. He agreed but, for reasons of safety, declined to do so until after the Meeting was over; it would be their secret until then. She said that at the dinner, he had a look of doom but laughed it out of his face, remarking that 'there are more ways of flying than dying'.

Although best known for the car company, Charlie Rolls was a racing driver, keen balloonist, self-taught pioneer aviator, occasional chauffeur in his Rolls-Royce for Queen Mary and much more besides. A local charity, the Charles Rolls Heritage Trust, has been formed with the object of advancing public education about Rolls and the Aviation Meeting.

Above left: Rolls as a racing driver. (Reproduced by permission of copyright holders)

Above right: Rolls and Wright Flyer. Early aviation was not for the faint-hearted. (Steve Robson)

Below: Hengistbury Head aerodrome of 1910. Rolls crashed near the starting line.

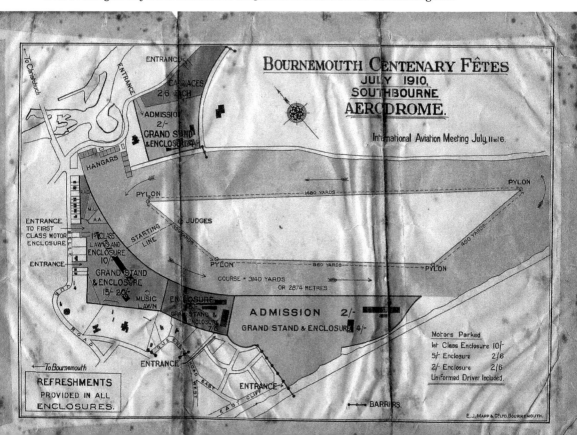

Russell-Cotes

In 1860, Merton Cotes (1835–1921) married Annie Clark (1835–1920) in Glasgow and they went on to have five children. From their first arrival in Bournemouth, Merton and his wife were enthusiastic supporters of the town, playing a major part in its governance and development.

In 1876, he understood the property potential of the Bath Hotel, purchasing it and moving his family into a suite of rooms on Christmas Day, quite a change after variously living in Wolverhampton, Glasgow, Buenos Aires and Dublin. Following substantial, Creeke-designed extensions financed by Annie, the hotel was reopened by the Lord Mayor of London in 1880 and renamed the Royal Bath.

Having built a house of great character within the hotel grounds as a birthday present to Annie by 1901, Cotes named it East Cliff Hall and the family moved in, sharing their huge collection of art, sculptures and oriental treasures with the hotel. Merton was mayor between 1894 and 1895.

Above: Bath Hotel (main building on left) and setting, *c.* 1858. (Mrs Julia Smith)

Right: Russell-Cotes distinctive family home, the former East Cliff Hall.

When knighted in 1909, becoming Sir Merton Russell-Cotes, he must have reflected on some of his and Annie's work promoting the town they loved: the Lansdowne clock, the London rail link via Brockenhurst, the non-commercialised Undercliff Drive, the gift of sculptures and paintings (including by Turner and Landseer) and the East Cliff Hall, which became a town museum after their deaths. Bournemouth has indeed been lucky in its benefactors.

Main Hall balcony of Russell-Cotes Art Gallery and Museum. (RCAGM)

S

Shelley's Heart: Gruesome Aftermath of Poet's Death

Percy Bysshe Shelley (1792–1822) was drowned at Viareggio, Tuscany, in a tragic boating accident when he and his two companions failed to cope in a bad storm.

The burial of Shelley in St Peter's churchyard includes only his heart, if that, the rest of the body having been cremated on the beach under quarantine law. After it was washed ashore and buried by local militia, it was exhumed and cremated by his friend Edward Trelawny (1792–1881), who also claimed to have rescued the heart from the funeral pyre.

However, there is doubt. Trelawny was notoriously unreliable and it is questionable whether it would have been possible to rescue the heart. Since the tomb's engraving does not mention Shelley's heart, its burial was presumably non-existent or unofficial, while the churchyard notice board lists 'heart only', as does a nearby blue plaque. Otherwise, Shelley's ashes are buried in Rome next to those of Trelawny, who purchased the adjacent plot in 1822.

Percy Bysshe Shelley by Alfred Clint, 1829, based on a work of 1819. (© National Portrait Gallery London)

When the poet's widow, Mary Wollstonecraft Shelley, the authoress of Frankenstein, was near death in 1851, she had a particular request of their son Sir Percy Florence Shelley. It was to be buried in a family tomb at St Peter's together with her parents, noted writers William Godwin and Mary Wollstonecraft, whose London remains therefore had to be exhumed.

On his death in 1889, Sir Percy was buried in the family tomb, reportedly together with his father's heart in a casket. Another opinion is that the heart was buried with Sir Percy's widow, Lady Jane Shelley who died in 1899. Yet the claim of Lady Abinger, the widow of Lady Jane's heir, may be the most likely: that Lady Jane's nephew, Canon M. W. F. St John, had persuaded her that the heart should be placed in the tomb, a task he carried out before her death, thus leaving an empty casket for the heir.

Southbourne's Challenge

As Bournemouth became a health resort, Doctor Thomas Armetriding Compton (1838–1925), whose medical practice was in the town centre, spotted the potential of land to the east. Apart from Cellars Farm and the farm-based villages of Tuckton and Wick, there were virtually no houses except Carbery, Heatherlea, Stourwood and Stourcliffe.

In 1871, he purchased 230 acres of cliff side land running from Clifton Road to Cellars Farm. The next year, he built Belle Vue Road from Carbery to Tuckton and relocated a glass house from Andover to create a popular winter garden 320 feet long at what is now Southbourne Crossroads. Flowers, fruit and vegetables were on sale, a horse operated a 120-foot-deep well and visitors came by regular horse omnibus from the town centre. Later, an assembly room for 400 was installed within one third of its length. By 1875, there were twenty-four bathing boxes on the beach.

Compton formed a development company to establish building plots, roads, pier, sea wall, promenade and six adjacent house terrace sites and promoted his estate as Southbourne-on-Sea. By 1881, Southbourne had forty-six houses and a twenty-two-bedroom hotel: the South Cliff. It was soon being advertised as one of the sunniest spots in England and described as 'in its infancy but a formidable rival to Bournemouth'. Churches, schools, shops and a post office were all built to satisfy demand.

Conditions were believed good for treating tuberculosis, asthma and anaemia, while the 1891 Brights' Guide talked about the valuable Chalybeate Spring, towards the western end of the promenade.

The Tuckton Bridge Company, which provided the first toll bridge in 1883 at a total cost of nearly £4,000, created a successful and profitable link to Christchurch. The 300-foot pier and landing stage opened in 1888 and Compton moved into one of the six new houses adjoining the promenade.

But not all was well, quite apart from the unrealistic idea of Southbourne rivalling Bournemouth. The pier and 1885-built upright sea wall by the promenade were seriously damaged by 1900–01 winter storms and never repaired through lack of funds. The terrace of six houses was wisely demolished and Southbourne was taken into Bournemouth County Borough in 1901.

When Compton gave evidence to a 1906 Bournemouth inquiry into sea walls, he suggested that the Southbourne one would have withstood the storms given three feet greater depth of concrete. Nonetheless, the Corporation decided on a sloping, not upright sea wall design for its important 1907 Undercliff Drive by Bournemouth Pier.

Although the winter garden, its assembly room, the original bridge, the hotel, the promenade and the pier have all now disappeared, the legacy remains: it was Doctor Compton who invented and established Southbourne.

Right: Tuckton Bridge, 1907, rebuilt for trams with reinforced concrete, 1905. (Alwyn Ladell)

Below: Wreck of Southbourne Pier thirteen years after opening in 1888. (Alwyn Ladell)

Wreck of Pier — Southbourne

Square, The

In the eighteenth century, the turnpike road linking Christchurch to Poole ran through The Brook, a location which is now the town centre. A ford crossed the water until the Bourn Plank was installed to help pedestrians, about the only building to be seen being Bourne House and Decoy Pond Cottage next door. When a footbridge was built in the middle of the nineteenth century, the area was called The Bridge but later renamed The Square.

As Bournemouth grew up on both sides of the marshy bottom of the valley, an improved link was needed. It was both natural and planned to turn the location of The Bridge into a wide area of level land accessed by radial roads and having the town's main buildings towards the bottom of the valley slopes. Great credit is due to the early landowners and Improvement Commissioners (1856–90) who ensured the continuing open layout of The Square within the green wedge of the Bourne Valley.

Today, it is a large and busy pedestrianised area including a café and space for stalls and outdoor entertainment, while also being close to many shops and bus stands, restaurants,

Elegant Square sees competition between horse and tram, early 1900s. (Alwyn Ladell)

Lamp standard maintenance, 1907. (Alwyn Ladell)

The Square today. Transformed, except for the NatWest building.

cinemas, a conference centre and the Town Hall. No longer is The Square frequented by horses and carriages, noisy trams, silent trolley buses or even the endless traffic around the previous huge ornamental garden of a roundabout with its central clock tower.

Sited as it is between the Middle and Lower Gardens, which have a gentle walk to the pier and the most popular central beach, The Square is a remarkable and attractive town centre.

Stevenson, Robert Louis

Stevenson (1850–94) did some of the best work of his short, troubled life during his three years at Bournemouth (1884–87), including *Strange Case of Dr Jekyll and Mr Hyde*, *Kidnapped*, and *A Child's Garden of Verses*.

Born in Edinburgh, son of the noted lighthouse engineer Thomas, he studied engineering but decided against it, becoming instead a barrister though he hardly practised as one. Finally, he insisted on the life of a writer. In Paris, Robert met and fell in love with Fanny Van de Grift Osbourne, a separated Californian woman. After her divorce, they married in San Francisco in 1880, spending the next winter in Switzerland as he battled with tuberculosis.

The 1884 move, with his family to temporary accommodation in Bournemouth, was again planned for health reasons after nearly dying in France earlier that year. He was very thin and wasted, coughed up blood and had relapses in the days before antibiotics. Yet throughout the pain and distress, he was often very positive. Perhaps Bournemouth did provide a new lease of life. He wrote:

> It blows an equinoctial gale, and has blown for nearly a week. Nimbus Britannicus, piping wind, lashing rain; the sea is a fine colour, and wind-bound ships lie at anchor under the Old Harry Rocks, to make one glad to be ashore.

At a time when RLS was very short of money, Thomas bought Fanny a Westbourne house, Sea View, which Robert renamed Skerryvore after the lighthouse built by his Uncle Alan off Argyll's coast. That year, artist J. S. Sargent painted him, remarking that Stevenson was 'the most intense creature I had ever met'.

On leaving in 1887, Stevenson suddenly felt he loved Skerryvore and Bournemouth, and burst into tears at the door as he said farewell to the housekeeper and the maid. Bombed on 16 November 1940, the house was demolished in 1941. In 1957, the council converted it into a memorial garden, No. 61 Alum Chine Road opposite R. L. Stevenson Avenue.

After Bournemouth, he travelled widely, eventually settling in Samoa until his death there due to a brain haemorrhage.

R. L. Stevenson by Sir William Blake Richmond, 1887. (© National Portrait Gallery London)

Talbot Village: Place of Benevolence and Self-help

In the nineteenth century, the wealthy Talbot sisters from London showed great concern for the area. The family having moved from Grosvenor Square and built Hinton Wood House on the East Cliff, Miss Georgina Talbot and her sister Marianne were very sympathetic to the poor who had banged on the windows saying they were starving and asking for work.

As a kind act of social reform for the unemployed, Georgina purchased 465 acres (0.73 square miles) at Wallisdown to create a Victorian self-supporting village. By 1870, the Talbot Model Village had six farms, seven almshouses (for seven old or infirm couples), nineteen three-bedroom cottages in 1-acre plots, St Mark's School for over sixty pupils and St Mark's Church. Actually, all of this land was in Poole until Bournemouth Corporation expanded in 1931 to annex 4,627 acres, which included that part of the Talbot land north of Wallisdown Road.

Georgina Charlotte Talbot.
(St Mark's School)

In 1870, Georgina died but Marianne continued the good work until her death in 1885. Key to the thinking was the requirement that tenants would be industrious working men who would only move out if they became wealthy. No workhouse for them.

Although some woodland and heath remain, most of the original site has changed with the times out of all recognition. It now incorporates two Bournemouth universities (both in Poole), a velodrome, more school lands, a large residential area, allotments and recreation areas. The Talbot Village Trust is a charity still concerned with the residual estate and having net assets in 2020 of some £67 million.

Tregonwells Ride Out and Buy Land: Bournemouth's Foundation Claim

In 1800, Lewis Dymoke Grosvenor Tregonwell (1758–1832) married his second wife, heiress Henrietta Portman. Tragically, seven years later, their infant son, Grosvenor, died from an accidental medical overdose, leaving his mother inconsolable and still dejected in 1810 when the couple were on holiday at the fashionable watering place of Mudeford.

Lewis suggested they ride out to Bourne, a beautiful valley that he knew from his days as a captain in the Dorset Volunteers Rangers, Cranborne Troop. Reportedly, they visited the recently built Tapps Arms. She was immediately charmed, seeing that it was a quiet, secluded spot with cliffs, sands and sea that would be ideal for a summer residence. Five years earlier, Sir George Ivison Tapps had purchased much of the valley under the Christchurch Inclosure Award and had built the Tapps Arms by 1809. The next year he agreed to sell to Tregonwell 8.5 acres for £179 11s in what is now Exeter Road. Actually, Tapps initially wanted to build holiday homes and in 1809 advertised to let a marine villa: Ashley Villa in what is now Old Christchurch Road. Tregonwell's second purchase in 1812, of the 4-acre Tapps Arms site, included at least two cottages, so explaining his reported reference in 1811 to 'Tapps' colony at Bourne'.

By 1812, Lewis had erected a cottage for his butler Symes and the Mansion House for his family. Little else was built around that time e.g. Cliff Cottage for

Lewis Tregonwell by Thomas Beach, 1798. (Mrs Julia Smith)

the Drax Grosvenor family who were old friends and Terrace Cottage for Lewis's gardener. While the Tregonwells, the Drax Grosvenors and their aristocratic friends enjoyed the tiny village of Bourne, there was no real wish to expand it for many years.

Lewis died in 1832 and Tapps in 1835. The latter's son and heir had different ideas, enabling significant building by 1838, thereby making the development of Bourne unstoppable. After Henrietta's death in 1846, her son John started to develop the Tregonwell land.

That ride on horseback from Mudeford to Bourne generated the land purchase claimed to demonstrate the 1810 foundation of Bournemouth as a watering place. Yet this perceived foundation was inadvertent because the Tregonwells did not want to start a new town, not in their time anyway.

Typhoid Epidemic

In 1936, Bournemouth, Christchurch and Poole suffered an outbreak of typhoid fever which was considered so serious that the eminent epidemiologist Doctor William Shaw, from the Ministry of Health, began his on-site investigation the day after notification on 21 August. Such was his extraordinary efficiency, remedial action was implemented the next day.

Shaw was informed that there had been thirty cases during the previous twenty-four hours, all with a common factor: consumption of raw milk from distributor Frowds of Poole. Having found no source of infection at the retailer's depot nor by blood tests among staff distributing the milk, the investigation centred on the supply from thirty-seven Dorset farmers.

The culprit proved to be a stream contaminated with human bacteria from the overflow of a storm water and sewage tank, located upstream at the grand Merley House in Wimborne. The proximity of the cows to the water caused the milk to become infected. The owner, ex-Etonian and ex-Conservative MP for South Dorset Captain Angus Hambro, was mortified to learn that he was the carrier having previously had typhoid without realising it.

Altogether, 718 contracted the disease, fifty-one died locally and at least twenty died further afield. One of the survivors was Peter Coles, who was just four in 1936 but went on to become a partner in Fox & Sons and Poole mayor in 1981.

The doctor required Frowds to pasteurise all milk after the morning round of 22 August. This was done, thereby immediately halting the outbreak, which was the worst milk-borne typhoid epidemic the country had known. Nonetheless, many thought the disaster had been handled too secretively, Frowds went into receivership and hotel bookings suffered badly.

Sadly in January 1937, Doctor Shaw died of pneumonia after influenza at the age of sixty-three.

UK's First Port and Town

Hengistbury Head's extraordinary prehistory embraces campsites from the Old Stone Age and the Middle Stone Age, followed by a Neolithic farming community. It was then used as a Bronze Age cemetery probably also including some human occupation, until Iron Age people built the Double Dykes to provide security for their town and port.

The first, or one of the first, true Iron Age towns in the country was centred on the low land east of the Dykes. After the settlement began around 700 BC, occupation

Port, Double Dykes, round houses, cattle pens and smelting on skyline at Hengistbury Head. (Illustrator Judith Dobie)

seems to have been limited and intermittent. However, once the port was established around 100 BC, it really thrived as one of the first trading links between Britain and the continent, until the Roman invasion of AD 43.

At that time, there were abundant ironstones on the beach enabling clifftop smelting and the manufacture of swords, nails, knives and farm implements. Activities and markets sprang up involving metalwork, spinning, weaving and cattle slaughter. Continental culture was imported with goods such as wine, figs, pottery and manganese glass, while various metal ores came in from the West Country. Exports included hides, cattle, craft ware, hunting dogs, corn, metal goods and slaves. The huge Bushe-Fox archaeological excavation of 1911–12 yielded a hoard of 3,000 coins.

The Dykes are about the only evident sign of the original bustling town, port and market.

United Reformed Church: A Bournemouth Evolution

When a Congregational Church was erected at Richmond Hill in 1856, the first appointed minister happened to be a Scottish Presbyterian who proceeded to introduce a Presbyterian approach to the life of the church. Since this led to some discontent, he resigned and in 1857 founded St Andrew's Church in a building of timber structure, clad in corrugated iron. Known as the Scotch Church and with a capacity of 320, it stood on the site of today's NatWest Bank in The Square.

St Andrew's was rebuilt in stone in 1872 but congregations continued to grow, leading to a sale for redevelopment as a hotel and relocation in 1888 to a larger new church in Exeter Road. Three years later, the Richmond Hill Congregational Church was also rebuilt.

In 1972, the Presbyterian Church combined with the Congregationalists as the United Reformed Church. From that time, therefore, Bournemouth had two centrally located URCs. Finally in 2005, when there was a ministerial vacancy, both churches combined at what is now known as Richmond Hill St Andrew's United Reformed Church.

Scotch Church at the foot of Richmond Hill in *c.* 1871. (Bournemouth Library)

Above: St Andrew's Church, Exeter Road, is now the Halo nightclub.

Left: Richmond Hill St Andrew's United Reformed Church of today.

V

Victoria Crosses

The highest military decoration for valour in the face of the enemy has been made posthumously to three Bournemouth men, as commemorated by inscription on the sculpture by Jonathan Sells in the grounds of the Bournemouth International Centre.

Cpl C. R. Noble (1891–1915) was fatally shot while cutting through barbed wire on the front line so that British troops could advance.

Sgt F. C. Riggs (1888–1918) was killed in action after capturing a machine gun, making fifty of the enemy surrender, and resisting to the last.

Lt Col D. A. Seagrim (1903–43) led an attack on two machine gun posts in Tunisia, accounting for twenty of the enemy, later dying from severe wounds in a military hospital.

There is a lot more to be said than is possible here about the extreme bravery shown by these men and the stories of their lives and deaths.

Sculpture of Tregonwell pays respect to three Bournemouth men awarded Victoria Crosses.

Westbourne: The Urban Village

Long ago, an attempt was made to provide alum for the whole of England by undercutting the price of imports. Although in 1567 Queen Elizabeth I granted Baron Mountjoy (1533–82) twenty-one years' monopoly rights for this dye fixative, little viable aluminous shale was ever found, the venture leading him to financial ruin but creating the name of Alum Chine.

In the 1860s, building began with some houses in large plots between Poole Road and Alum Chine and continued with shops around Seamoor Road. Branksome Dene was erected in 1860 towards the sea end of Alumhurst Road and extended in 1880 and 1913, finally becoming a Masonic care home with a change of name to Zetland Court. In its time, it has been a marine mansion owned by Lord Wimborne and later Lady Edwina Mountbatten before use as a hotel for vegetarians.

Methodist Church became Tesco in 2010 – welcome adaptation or incongruity?

Henry Joy's arcade of 1884 is crowded and bustling.

Right: Delightful tropical gardens of Alum Chine laid out in the 1920s.

Below: Alum Chine playground dedicated to R. L. Stevenson. *Inset*: A partly opened treasure chest.

After Bournemouth West station opened in 1874, development was even faster and ten years later, Westbourne became part of Bournemouth. Other key features include the Grand Cinema Theatre (1922) and the Royal Victoria Hospital (1887).

The village has adapted to the closure of the station (1965) and the hospital (in 2002 for conversion to apartments), while the Grand was used for bingo until its closure in 2019. Perhaps the biggest modern change is the sale of many houses in large plots to build flats. Yet this western suburb, close to the town centre, retains its individuality and character.

Westover Road Then and Now: Bond Street of Bournemouth

From 1836 to 1838, the tiny village of Bourne witnessed a major and unprecedented property development comprising the Belle Vue Boarding House, the Bath Hotel and sixteen villas in the brand new Westover Road.

Westover Road villas, two hotels, church and sheep in 1842. (Bournemouth Library)

Much of the eastern villa remains visible adjoining the later front extension in mock-Tudor style.

Although a few dwellings had been erected since that first visit of the Tregonwells in 1810, here was the first major sign of a new resort with an effective road network. Westover Road now linked The Square and the Bath Hotel, so opening up the potential of the town centre and the East Cliff. A measure of that potential is the high density of the subsequent commercial redevelopment of the Westover Road apartment houses and residences.

Thus, however delightful the wooded setting of the Westover Villas, they were destined for complete demolition, except for the eastern one (number sixteen), which became part of a hotel.

Winter Gardens

In 1877, a huge steel and glass structure was erected on the west side of Exeter Road in Cranborne Gardens. The Winter Gardens were born, boasting a lounge, reading room, stalls, buffets and concert hall where fêtes could be attended and the piano or draughts could be played.

The site had previously been enjoyed by the Tregonwells as landowners and after widow Henrietta's death in 1846, there was even archery. Later, it was partly developed

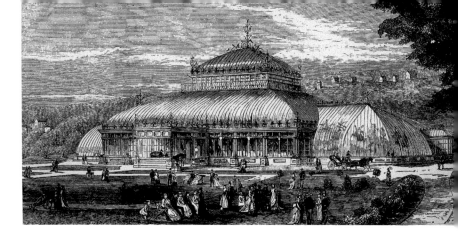

Winter Gardens – a Victorian paradise? Artist's engraving from *c.* 1880.

Winter Gardens indoor bowling centre by Eustace Nash, 1937. (Mrs Myrna Chave)

as a roller-skating rink. Although the new venue hosted a grand illuminated fête with Japanese lanterns and even a circus, it did not catch on, falling into disuse by 1892.

The Corporation brought in an Italian band, did some renovations and finally employed bandmaster Dan Godfrey, who opened to great and ongoing success in May 1893. His well-run and talented Bournemouth Municipal Orchestra was homed at the Gardens among the decorative plants, so ensuring musical fame for the town and effective use of a building that could hold 4,000.

Once the Bournemouth Pavilion was completed in 1929, the orchestra was relocated, the glass gardens being demolished and rebuilt in brick by 1937 as an indoor bowling green. Ten years later after its conversion to a concert hall, the Winter Gardens again hosted the orchestra, becoming famous for excellent acoustics and a great variety of entertainment, including for example George Formby, the Beatles, Eartha Kitt and Maurice Chevalier.

By 2006, the Winter Gardens were considered past their time and despite strong opposition were demolished for a car park. In September 2020, 378 flats were approved on the 4.9-acre site together with a commercial and leisure scheme (of *c.* 66,000 square feet) and 522 car spaces. The orchestra is now based at Poole Lighthouse, Bournemouth no longer being the same home to music as it was in Godfrey's day. Sad indeed.

World War Two's Worst Air Raid

Long after the Blitz had ended, Bournemouth suffered its most damaging attack, being number forty-eight out of the fifty raids reported by the end of 1943. It lasted for one minute, during which 11 tons of high-explosive bombs were dropped.

Around 1 p.m. on Sunday 23 May 1943, twenty-six Focke-Wulf 190 fighter-bombers flew in at low level for a hit-and-run operation, which included machine-gunning airmen and others in the Pleasure Gardens. Records show that twenty-two bombs hit their targets, destroying twenty-two buildings with another thirty-seven requiring demolition and 3,422 being damaged. Major direct hits included the Central Hotel and Punshon Memorial Church at the bottom of Richmond Hill, the Metropole Hotel at the Lansdowne and Beales Department Store.

There were seventy-seven civilians killed and 196 injured. Total military deaths of all nationalities were later disclosed to be 131.

Pilot Karl Schmidt, at the age of twenty-one, was shot down by a machine gun post on the roof of the East Cliff Court Hotel. His aircraft crashed into the St Ives Hotel, No. 34 Grove Road with an intact bomb, which did not at first explode. Another German flier died after his damaged aircraft's wing was caught in a tree when landing at Caen, causing the plane to cartwheel. Later that day the Municipal Orchestra, conducted by Adrian Boult, played Elgar's 'Nimrod' from the *Enigma Variations* in tribute to those who had died. That night 826 aircraft from Bomber Command bombed Dortmund. 'Bournemouth is certainly a legitimate objective, packed with soldiers and airmen as it is' (Diary of Australian airman, 1942).

Above: Royal London House was built on the Metropole site.

Left: Metropole Hotel, Lansdowne, after 1943 raid and WVS supporting rescuers. (Bournemouth Library)

Xenophobia, Bournemouth Style

The early days of the health resort were exclusively for the well-off and those who provided the necessary services. From its time as a playground for Tregonwell and his aristocratic friends to its development as a watering place for the rich and those wanting health cures, it was all very select. Then the railway arrived.

Once it became possible for people of all classes (as the residents saw it) to make day trips and visit the beach, there was understandable tension. The *Bournemouth Echo* of 20 August 1900 takes up the story in this extract:

> At present we are in the grip of the 'tripper' season. The day tripper is generally intent on getting his money's worth. He now comes vast distances from the grimy northern towns; the railways bring him and the female of the species at reduced rates. When he is gone, select high-class Bournemouth hurriedly clears his luncheon papers and empty bottles from her beach and pleasure grounds and breathes more freely. But it is not until the short tripping season is over that our town resumes its wonted air of respectability and awakens to a superior kind of life. Then begin to arrive the higher class of winter residents.

Yellow Buses and Their Forebears

Public transport began in 1851 with two horse-drawn omnibuses, each running twice a day from the Bath Hotel, one to Poole Station and one to Holmsley Station. Trams ran from 1902 to 1936, trolley buses from 1933 to 1969 and motor buses from 1906 to today.

Councillors initially felt that trams were wrong for the town's elegant image, but eventually relented provided they were 'to Bournemouth standard' and run by the Corporation. Technology advanced and a successful 1933 trial of four trolley buses proved they were quicker, quieter, cheaper, less obstructive and safer for passengers. It was not to last. By 1969, few trolley bus manufacturers were left and spares were difficult, while the greatly improved motor buses coped better and more cheaply with altered roads, especially the Wessex Way which was unsuited to overhead wires.

The 1950 performance of 64 million journeys remains a record, the later decline being due to factors like petrol derationing, more private motoring, TV and five-day weeks. Buses faced more congestion while the fewer passengers suffered increased journey times. There are currently some 150 buses based at Yeoman's Way and about 15 million journeys per annum.

In 1982, feedback was sought about the name. The reply, 'Why not Yellow Buses? That's what we always say', was adopted. Indeed, it has been a predominant colour since the days of the trams starting with primrose and since 2006, becoming a brighter shade.

In 1986, transport assets were transferred to Bournemouth Transport Ltd, a profitable independent company, albeit owned by the council. After a sale to Transdev in 2005 and resale to RATP in 2011, there was another resale in 2019 via a management buyout, which delighted the purchasers. Now that the managers are masters of their own destiny, local control has returned.

1978 Leyland Fleetline paddle steamer with removable roof. (D. L. Chalk, Bournemouth Transport Ltd)

Zamek Brothers: Bournemouth Heroes Recognised by the Name Zamek Close, Kinson

At 21.10 hours on 2 October 1940, an aircraft, powered by the excellent Rolls-Royce Merlin engines, took off from an RAF station near York to bomb a power station near Frankfurt.

At the age of twenty-two, Sgt Observer Ian Zamek of the RAF Volunteer Reserve was killed together with the rest of the five aircrew when their Whitley Type V, Serial N1434 Code GE-E of 58 Squadron, crashed without survivors. Ian is believed to be the only Jewish boy from Bournemouth buried in the Commonwealth War Cemetery in Berlin. His fellow airmen are in the same cemetery.

Whitley bomber. (© Airfix, wholly trademark owned by Hornby Hobbies Ltd, 2020)

Z

At the age of twenty during air operations against the Japanese in Burma on 16 July 1942, his brother Sgt Pilot Norman Zamek, also of the Reserve, died on active duty when flying his Hurricane fighter of 135 Squadron. His grave is in the Ranchi Cemetery some 260 miles north-west of Calcutta (Kolkata since 2001).

Acutely aware of the risks, Norman had written to his parents two months earlier about the shock that he knew would be caused by bad news. He said that he 'can think of no greater use for my life than helping to defend the cause for which we are now fighting'. It is hard to imagine their feelings when they heard of his death.

Zoo at Charminster

Although Gerald Durrell (1925–95) was keen to have a proper Bournemouth zoo, discussions with the council proved difficult and eventually in 1959, he founded one in Jersey. He argued that a zoo would be an attraction in any town, but said 'to judge by the way they reacted, one would have thought that I wanted to set off an atomic bomb on one of the piers!' For a time, Upton House, Poole, was considered suitable, but negotiations failed.

Hence, Durrell's Bournemouth zoo aspirations were limited to a house garden in Charminster and on one occasion, the premises of J. J. Allen near St Peter's Church.

His widowed mother Louisa, and her four children, had left India for England in 1928, moving from London to Parkstone and finally to Wimborne Road, Bournemouth, in 1932. The idyllic, televised Corfu story began with Gerald's brother Lawrence persuading Louisa to emigrate in 1935 and ended with a forced return to England in 1939 to avoid the nightmare of fascism under Mussolini.

Louisa bought a family house in St Alban's Avenue, Bournemouth, and Gerald's sister, Margot, purchased a boarding house opposite. It is still there, a substantial double-fronted two-storey house, currently arranged as five flats. Animal collecting, financed by an inheritance, began just after the war when he brought crates of them back to his sister's property. He was living there in a small attic flat and writing books to finance more expeditions, while tending his unofficial zoo in the garden.

The arrangement with J. J. Allen, which was a Christmas publicity stunt involving Durrell's Menagerie meeting the public, did have one problem: the Sunday escape of Georgina the baboon from the well-appointed basement with its roomy cages and foliage murals. Churchgoers were reportedly amazed and shocked to see Georgina going through a window furniture display like a tornado!

Bournemouth's loss was Jersey's gain.

About the Author

Bill Hoodless is a retired chartered surveyor who has mainly lived in Bournemouth since his family moved here from Upminster in 1948 when he was one year old. He feels a great affinity for his home town and particularly wanted to make this contribution to the story of its heritage.

Retirement gives the chance to concentrate on those things that are not always possible, such as the joys of writing. Yet perhaps 'joys' is not the right word when one considers the amount of time necessarily denied to one's long-suffering family.

This is Bill's eighth book and the first one published by Amberley. The first, published by the Poole Historical Trust in 2005, concerned Hengistbury Head and the next was about the Essex Blitz. Two followed about Christchurch, then Bournemouth Curiosities, Brexit and finally, Charles Rolls and the First Bournemouth Air Show of 1910.